The Many Lives of Zillah Smith:
An English Romany

The Many Lives of Zillah Smith
An English Romany

Netta Cartwright

Edited by
Katherine Mulraney

YOUCAXTON PUBLICATIONS
OXFORD & SHREWSBURY

Published in 2016 by YouCaxton Publications

ISBN 978-1-911175-19-3

For Tina Marie, Aleisha, Mary, John and Kath

In Memoriam

Dr. Katherine Mulraney

June 1st 1974 - September 1st 2016.

Acknowledgments

I would like to express my gratitude to everyone who has helped me write this book. I especially appreciate my husband David Pinnock, who has been a constant source of support throughout my journey of producing this book, not least in terms of being so patient about my use of our office over the years. I would like to give my heartfelt thanks to my daughter the late Dr. Katherine Mulraney for her editing and proofreading of the manuscript. Her long standing enthusiasm for the project, her steadfast encouragement and sharing of expertise in Roma studies has been not only invaluable but most of all inspiring. I would like to give special thanks to my readers in the penultimate stages of the book namely, Roy Samson, Jonathan Pinnock, Joan Michelson, Professor Liz Doherty and Pat Sanderson. They provided me with much needed encouragement in these latter stages as well as wise and practical suggestions on how to enhance it. I am also very grateful to Julie Wells for the final proofread and greatly appreciate and commend Bob Fowke and Steve Edwards at YouCaxton Publishing for their professional assistance and expertise. Finally, and most importantly, I am hugely indebted and endlessly grateful to the Smith family especially Grace Smith and of course Zillah herself. They have given me so much of their time and energy over the years including many hours of discussion, laughter and tears, providing the memories, the stories, the poems and the wonderful photographs.

I have gathered facts and information wherever possible from published sources including books and official census returns as well as drawing on the recollections of Zillah and several members of her extended family. I have done my best to reference all sources including the photographs and to ensure that all names, places and dates are correct. If there are any mistakes in this respect these are mine alone and please accept my apologies.

Contents

List of Illustrations

The following are all family photographs apart from some externally sourced as labelled. Those indicated by* are photographs taken by the author.

Prologue

" The river was me looking glass "

"Me name's Boswell," she said, "but I'm a Lee. Me name's Sarah Smith but I was a Boswell. I was born Zillah Boswell and some people call me Sarah but you can call me Zillah Smith. Me 'usband's mother was a Lee and we 'ad a bit of a struggle because you didn't 'ave much in them days y'know. But we got married young just after me sixteenth birthday come up. We went an' got married in a registry office. I 'ad a hard life with me family an' I 'ad a lot o' children, thirteen altogether. An' I brought 'em all up. Everyone says what a lovely family they are. I give 'em all me love an' that's as far as I can go. All that I live for is me children an' grandchildren. They're all brought up the right way an' I've 'ad a hard life bringin' 'em up. They never 'ad what they got today. I washed me hair in rainwater and the river was me lookin' glass. We made us our own pegs an' flowers. We got willow and cedar wood for 'em out o' Gypsy forests an' Gypsy woods an' went callin' and sellin' to keep the children when I had 'em small. We just 'ad to live day by day and I looked after 'em the best way I could. But I'm proud o' me children y'know an' I'm proud o' me Gypsy life."

Picture 2: Zillah at my house in the late 1980s.

The woman before me smiling and looking me straight in the eye was a complete picture of Romany self-esteem. She declared it with her gold earrings and her mother and grandmother's thick golden rings on her fingers. It showed in her Gypsy hairstyle with waves patted and combed into place with a little oil to get them just right. I could see it in her choice of wares for sale - some elastic and lace, a lucky black cat brooch, a small bouquet of paper flowers; and a pair of rose earrings.

She'd come knocking on my door one January morning in 1988 and could probably tell I saw her as a friendly Gypsy who was not short of stories and some fortunes to tell. Indeed I felt lucky to meet her and was full of curiosity. I invited her in and she settled down for a cup of tea and an interested listener to her story. I still remember with a smile those opening words, laced from the start with ambiguity.

After that first meeting it was just a matter of weeks before Zillah returned to my door. This time, though, her face was sad and drawn, her voice the same but less spirited. She had something to tell me and cried for a long time in my arms. Her second youngest daughter Tina Marie was dead at the age of just 27 years leaving behind three small children.

This was when I began the writing of Zillah's story. She wanted her daughter's story to be told, and her own story before that. Tales delving back through the century and skipping forward to the new one were waiting to be told: times of Gypsy fortunes and misfortunes. Zillah had chosen me to write her story. She could not read or write herself and believed I had the skills to put down on paper what she could remember and the willingness and vision to make her stories come alive. She told me that, "My mind's clear. I can remember everything in the past and the future."

The writing of Zillah's story has been a journey in itself. Yet, like her, I feel that her story is important and for the telling. This journey to tell this story has spanned 28 years. It began with a Romany woman asking a non-Gypsy woman she barely knew to tell her story and has since included countless hours, days, months and years of conversation, story telling, writing, reading out and redrafting of manuscripts. Zillah's memories and stories started as far back as she could remember with both sets of her grandparents. Over the years we have become very good friends and met many of each other's families. I have met and interviewed most of her children, several grandchildren and great grandchildren. Her daughters Mary and Grace and even her great granddaughter Abigail have written their own accounts, which I have incorporated into the book.

Now that Zillah is in her 91st year it is time for the journey to end here with the publication of this book. It tells the story of a Romany woman and the many lives she has lived. Drawing on her memories over six generations, this story dates from the early 1800s to the present day. It shows a life lived in one of the most transformative centuries in British history. Zillah's story gives us a glimpse of a life long gone but also shows how many Romany Gypsy traditions still live on. Indeed, for me, perhaps what is most intriguing about this story is what it has to tell us all about the power of memories, community and family in helping to keep identities and traditions alive. Through her eyes we also learn about love, death, loss, the way we all live our lives and what it means to be human.

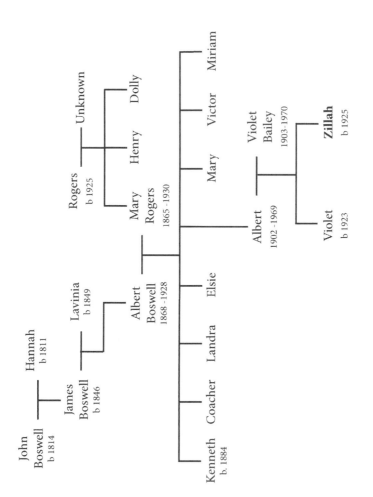

Picture 3 The Boswell Family Tree 1811-1930

Chapter 1

Zillah now and when it all began (1811-1930)

"No money getting up from nowhere if Gypsies didn't earn it."

Zillah's 90th birthday had finally arrived on March 20th 2015. Sitting in her family's favourite pub, she was surrounded by her family womenfolk, young and old, many of whom had travelled far and wide to celebrate this remarkable day. One of Zillah's daughters, Grace, had spring-cleaned her trailer first thing that morning whilst her other daughters had taken her to the hairdresser. Sitting at the head of the table Zillah was now resplendent in a long turquoise gown looking every inch the Matriarch. The assembled daughters and cousins were tucking into large helpings of a carvery roast lamb dinner with all the trimmings, roast 'taters, mint sauce, peas and gravy. Her daughters were excited as they had a nice surprise for Zillah later. As well as spring-cleaning her trailer, they had also given it a make-over decorating it with new rugs and ornaments. The day was everything she had hoped for.

Picture 4: Zillah's 90th birthday with daughters and some cousins, Stafford March 20th 2015

What a good mood everyone was in! Zillah had survived a hard winter; Grace and her husband Riley's family were secure for another three years to stay living on their small piece of land near Stratford; summer was coming with plenty of work for John, Zillah's youngest son, and her other sons; and Grace's granddaughter Abigail, Zillah's great great grandchild, was looking forward to going to secondary school near Stratford.

Picture 5: Zillah at Glover Street 2015

On returning to the Glover Street Gypsy Caravan site Zillah was delighted to see a new pot of beautiful daffodils and hyacinths next to the door of her trailer. The council site didn't have many flowers nowadays so it was a lovely springtime touch to what were otherwise bare and empty surroundings. The site was tucked away out of sight behind the large Sainsbury's supermarket in Stafford. It was easily missed and few people in Stafford knew it was there. In the past it was secured by a gate that Dempsey, her brother, the unpaid warden and licensee, had used to lock every night at about 10 o'clock in the evening. Now Elvis his son did it. Inside the gate was a wide road bordered on the left by a row of 12 plots behind fences each with a locked gate. Each plot had room for a large trailer and a permanent outhouse block housing a small working and storage area with sink and running water and a separate toilet and shower cubicle.

At the time of Zillah's birthday nearly all of the plots were empty. Despite a waiting list, no trailers were allowed onto the vacant sites. A few months previously the trailer of Olive, Zillah's sister-in-law, caught fire, and though her nephew had quickly doused the flames, the Council decided to close down the site to any new applicants and to reopen it with fewer but larger plots for safety reasons. Elvis was applying to take over the licence and take charge of its renovation when the council eventually re- open it but progress is slow due to lack of funding. Meanwhile, the months went by, the weeds grew taller and no new families could move in. Apart from the few plastic plants outside the few remaining trailers the site was a drab, monochrome, cold, and dreary place. In previous years the site had always been full of colour with beautiful plants and flowers on display and washing flapping in the wind. So Zillah's birthday daffs and hyacinths offered a welcome splash of colour.

After more celebrations the family eventually left Zillah to go to bed and think her own thoughts. March was always a difficult month for Zillah. She called it the month of the bavel (wind). Although it was her birthday month, for her it

Picture 6: Traditional Burning of a Gypsy Wagon at a Gypsy Funeral

was a time of sorrow. Her daughter Tina Marie was buried in March 1988 and now she was grieving for Dempsey her last brother who had died just 6 months before. As was the case for all her life and those before her, death was never far away. As far back as her memories could take her, kept alive through stories told to her by her parents and their parents, she would often revisit her family from years gone by.

One of the most striking memories that Zillah still carried with her was that of her own Granny's funeral on Sound Common. As a small chav (child) sitting on her mother Violet's knee she could still see the flames of her Granny Mary's varda[1] (horse drawn Gypsy caravan) shooting up into a black starry sky. Little Zillah, who had hazy comfortable feelings of times in the varda with her Granny, couldn't really understand why this precious home and her lovely things should go up in flames. It was the old Gypsy tradition her mother had explained.

Even then the tales told to little Zillah of her ancestors felt like conjuring up a life long gone. She was told of how her great grandparents born in the mid 1800s couldn't afford vardas so they slept in benders (tents) made out of hazel twigs covered with canvas. If they had no benders they would sleep beneath the tilt (canopy) of the cart. They begged for a lot of their clothes in those days but when they could afford it the men would buy a tailor made suit.

Zillah could remember her Granny Mary's "nice bender, her cooking and feeding me and the other chavvies in it". She imagined them in earlier days on foot travelling down the lanes using carts to carry their possessions. Zillah knew that her Great Granny Lavinia Boswell and her Granny Mary Rogers Boswell, both born in Staffordshire, travelled up and down with donkeys and lived in benders. It was only towards the turn of the 20th century that some families could begin to afford horses, ponies and vardas.

Zillah picked up from an early age that there was, "No money getting up from nowhere if Gypsies didn't earn it". They had had to learn to live from day to day and Zillah still often thought how that was a nice way to live. Zillah, however, also learned early on how important it was for Gypsies to develop and use skills to better their conditions. Her paternal grandfather, Albert, was the son of James and Lavinia Boswell who married in the early 1840s.

Zillah had dim memories of watching her granddad Albert stitching pieces of soft leather into shoes and listening to stories of his father James's life. He told her that his dad was one of the first shoemakers to make left and right feet and up till then all pairs of shoes were the same shape. Her great grandfather was a cordwainer (shoemaker) and passed on the skill to his son Albert. James born in 1846 had learnt his trade as a teenager in Northampton, a town dominated by shoemaking for centuries. He eventually moved North in the late 1860s making a living by his trade in Alsager's Bank and Halmer End near Audley situated in the rolling hills of North Staffordshire. Zillah's granddad told her that shoemaking was not the same as shoe mending, which was the job of a cobbler. The Cordwainer's job was more skilled and his father James ended up a relatively well off rom (Gypsy man) with high social standing in the Gypsy hierarchy of the time.

This branch of the Gypsy Boswells can be traced back to James's father John Boswell, who, born in 1814, went on to marry Hannah, James's mother and when they were travelling in the Northampton area they sent their son James (Zillah's great grandfather) to be an apprentice shoemaker with the Gorgias (non – Gypsy house dweller). Zillah remembered through stories passed down to her how her dad's family the Boswells had always been respectable, skilful and proper Romanies who were keen to better themselves. They looked like proper Romanies too being very dark in appearance. She remembered that Granddad Albert had dark skin and black hair even in his old age. He was what was known as a 'kushti mush' - a fine looking man.

As well as coming from a good-looking stock, his turn out was very smart with a clean shirt and brightly patterned neckerchief. As a small girl she was impressed when Granddad changed from his working leather waistcoat to an embroidered one for special occasions. She knew that he had a reputation for taking a pride in everything that he did. His donkeys and horses were beautifully groomed and their harnesses always polished.

Picture 7: Caricature of a "broomstick-wedding", from a two-penny sheet by James Catnach, The Marriage Act Displayed in Cuts and Verse, London, 1822.

Zillah had often heard the story of how her Granddad Albert had met Granny Mary in the early 1880s when they were still just teenagers. Both of them had come from highly respected Gypsy families but because they were still classed as chavs (children) and too young to marry Albert ran away with Mary to marry secretly.

According to tradition Mary was at first scolded by her family but they straightaway welcomed Albert and told the couple to come back and jump the broomsticks.[2] This was an old fashioned Gypsy wedding where the bride and bridegroom jumped over a whole flowering shrub called broom or over a broom made of hazel wood and birch twigs. Zillah didn't know which but she didn't think they'd gone as far as a blood wedding.

"In me great granny's day they used to cut their hands and jump the broomsticks around a stick fire but not very often. It'd only be the odd one that'd let the blood drip in like. But they used to have the old vardas around the outside against the big fire an' have a real nice do over it. All the Gypsy women cooked food for the wedding fare and it went on for days. Dad told me about it. His mam had told him."

Members of the Rogers and Boswells came from as far afield as Hereford, Peterborough and Wales to be at her grandparents' wedding.

After the wedding, Albert and Mary were able to purchase a Reading varda a particularly sought after big four-wheeler square wagon that was named after the town where it was built. It had narrow floors between tall wheels so they could safely cross over fords and rough ground. It had windows at the side and back and had sloping walls with portable steps leading up to the front door. A chimney poked out on the right from the bowed roof keeping clear of the hedges and overhead bridges. Zillah particularly remembered the carved and painted lion's head at the front of it.

Picture 8: Historic image of a traveller family, Reading varda and horse

They had to keep two good trustworthy horses for pulling the two ton wagon. One horse was for pulling while the other was in reserve and to change over.

Albert and Mary eventually went on to have seven children with most of them born before World War I. Zillah's father Albert was their fifth child born in 1901. His older brothers and sister were Kenneth, Coacher, Landra, and Elsie. In those pre-war years Albert and Mary and their young family travelled mostly with Albert's side of the family dealing horses in the North Midlands, sometimes as far as Appleby in Cumbria and Doncaster in Yorkshire. During the fruit picking season, they also travelled with Mary's relatives further south through Lichfield and Henley-on-Arden on the way to Evesham.

The seasons soon passed with the children of the family, including Zillah's father, often put to work from the age of four or five years. Boys cleaned the harnesses, groomed the animals and helped maintain the wagons. Girls fed the animals, cleaned the wagons, black leaded the tyres and varnished the wood. The girls and smaller boys went out with their mothers and aunts hawking and fortune telling and the boys stayed with their fathers making shoes (if they had the leather) or repairing them, grinding scissors, collecting scrap, and ferreting out rats on the farms. At the fairs, when they'd done their turn on the peg and basket stalls, the children were allowed to wander around to spend a few pence on some toffee apples and to enjoy the fair. Back at the camp the chavs played "Romnis and Roms" (wives and husbands) shouting, arguing and laughing like the grown-ups or pretending to go hawking by picking flowers, berries and nuts for food to bring home. Zillah liked to imagine how they might even have roasted some potatoes on a small stick fire and perhaps a bird one of the boys had catapulted or a fish tickled by one of the girls.

The men of the family also had to maintain a presence at the camp to pack up and move on at short notice when the gavvers (police) invariably showed up. Like all Gypsy families Albert and Mary's family had come to accept this and the men often harnessed the horses and moved on leaving a sign with long stalks of grass laid as arrows on the hedges pointing the right direction for the women on their return from a day's work.

Always being on the move made schooling difficult. Zillah often reflected on how schooling back then must have been as hard as it was for her and her children and grandchildren. She had heard stories of how her parents, uncles and aunts – those that did go to school - had to make out they were older than they were in order to avoid being put in with the younger classes. When they got in the right age class it was not much better. They were often getting into fights with the Gorgia children and being punished when it wasn't their fault. Zillah's dad, aunts and uncles had to wear dunces caps and stand in the corner or worse still have the cane sometimes just because they couldn't read something, answered back or worst of all talked to each other in their Romany Jib (language).

Zillah liked to think the Gypsy way of life back then was probably the best education for them. Away from school they were as fit as fiddles, close to nature and learning everything that was necessary for their survival and more. They learnt through living and playing: solving problems using their own wits or watching how the older ones did it. Their toys were marbles, peg tops, cardboard boxes, pieces of string, old wheels, tin cans, old bits of broken pots, left over bits of wood and anything else that came to hand.

As little Albert Junior and his siblings grew older their working roles grew and they regularly went out with the adults in the fields to pick fruit, peas and potatoes. The family lived hand to mouth from one day to the next. The winters were especially hard with family stories passed down about huge drifts of snow covering the benders and vardas. From her own experiences Zillah knew that in the varda they would have huddled around the Queenie stove (a wood burning stove)[3] and in the bender around a stick fire with smoke filling the tent and eventually drifting out through a hole in the roof. If they were lucky they had coal or coke but most commonly would have relied on wood.

Before the war Granny Mary and the other women spent their days hawking (selling) door to door with their donkeys and carts around the Cheshire and Staffordshire villages and made a decent enough living. They had all sorts for sale from small items they and the men had made such as paper flowers, clothes pegs to sometimes leather shoes, brooms and brushes. They also bought to sell on lace handkerchiefs, jewellery, ribbons as well as selling larger goods such as home made wicker baskets, repaired chairs, carpets, rugs and coconut mats. They usually had a few of the younger children with them and more often than not babies wrapped in a Welsh blanket[4] on their hips. The older children minded the donkeys while their mothers went around the houses and shops with the smaller ones.

Winter usually meant having to live nearer the bigger towns of Chester, Stoke, Stafford, Lichfield and Walsall to gain easier access to houses and a wider pool of potential customers. Here they found the town dwellers to be less friendly and more suspicious than the country people. The "townies" crossed the palms of Gypsies' hands with silver out of fear of being cursed whereas the country people didn't see much difference between themselves and the Gypsies who were just another lot of hardworking folk. In fact the great houses and farmers often welcomed their skills such as ferreting out rats.

During this time houses like Shugborough Hall, Goldstone Hall and Hanstall Hall provided work for Gypsy men back at their camps. For example housekeepers or butlers sometimes gave Mary and other Gypsy women worn out chairs to be repaired or cane bottoms to be put in. Mary loaded them on the cart and took them back to be mended for the following week.

With the onset of the First World War the lives of the Gorgios and that of Zillah's family would become ever more closely entwined. Zillah's father Albert and his elder brother Landra were both conscripted during the First World War. Landra was one of the first conscripts called up on January 10th 1916, aged just eighteen years old. At the time he had been living in a caravan in Fenton, in the Staffordshire Potteries and was working as a horse dealer and an ovenman, the most dangerous job in the Potteries. Landra had to place the pottery in the kilns and remove them after firing. It was heavy labour in extreme heat and if any pottery pieces were dropped he wouldn't get paid. Working in such drastic temperature changes also brought dangerous risks to the body.

Landra liked horses so he probably felt this change of "career" might bring him into more contact with them and was glad to get away from the ovens. By April 6th and now based in Lichfield he was appointed to the 4th Battalion of the Duke of Wellington in the Yorkshire Lancashire Regiment and dispatched to France. As part of the 4th Division his Battalion arrived just in time to play a valuable part at the battle of Le Cateau[5] after which his family assumed he remained on the Western Front throughout the war. His battalion took part in most of the major actions, including the battles of the Somme, Arras and Ypres though his family got no news of him or Albert.

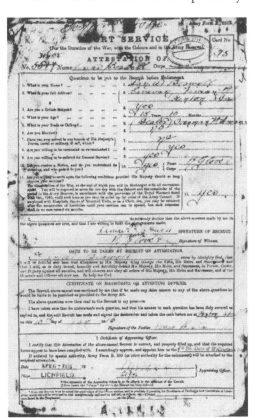

Picture 9: Landra's War Attestation, April 6th 1916

Grandfather Albert and Granny Mary did their best while Landra and Albert were away in France. Life down the lanes continued as before but it was leaner times. By this time Granny Mary, had had two more girls Mary and Miriam who were barely 12 and 8 years. The girls saw to the menfolk and looked after the washing and cooking so Granny Mary could go out hawking with the other women. During the First World War, this was their main source of income, but everything was scarce for Gorgios and Romanies alike. Women brought back less and less as the months and years wore on. Sometimes Mary and the others came back wet and cold after a whole day hawking with not even enough for a dinner that night. Similarly while there was work available on the farms, the pay was very low and the Boswell family could rarely earn enough to sustain a living for long.

Despite all of this, hawking in the villages and towns proved a valuable way of keeping Granny Mary and others informed about the war. One of the many hurts of the war for Romany families was that most of their soldier sons could not write. As far as Zillah knew the family never received news from either Albert or Landra from France while they were away. Albert returned safely though injured. "He got wounded in his arm and all the sinews in his arm went and they put rabbits' veins in them so 'e told me."

Landra never returned and they never had his body. It was said that Uncle Landra had had his head blown off when he was riding a horse in one of the battles. The loss of their son Landra broke the hearts of Granny Mary and Grandad Albert and while it was something often alluded to, his death was rarely talked about.

When thinking about the family's story of Landra's terrible death- how his parents never recovered from their grief and how they couldn't settle not having a body or a grave - Zillah was reminded of a story often told to her as a child. It was told of the fear of losing a son to the wicked ways of the devil. Her father told her about a Gypsy boy who was tricked by the devil into selling his soul. It was a fantastical story told as though true. His own father had told it to him when he was a boy. In fact it was a well-known tale as Zillah's future husband Ivor also had it told to him by his Uncle Slatter. (Appendix 4)

Zillah's youngest uncles, Bertie then aged 14 and Victor aged 10 would have had to have grown up even faster during this lean time, learning how to grind scissors, groom and breed the horses, train the dogs, mend and make the wagons and all the other jobs in the life of a Romany man. Their father and their elder brothers, Kenneth and Coacher, too old to be called up, would have been their teachers. For Granddad Albert now nearly 50 years old there would have been no possible way of doing things other than with horses or animals. He would have had no time at all for any of the new machines or mechanical forms of transport, including bicycles, that were now becoming commonplace. For him horses were everything and as a dealer he would have known how to look out for all the tricks of the trade when it came to buying and selling. This was something he could warn his sons about but could not teach. His sons learned by observing and copying their father at auctions. They soon picked up what to look for in a horse; the way it tensed its shoulder muscles, how it carried its head or moved its tail. They would need to identify along with their father any tricksters and any horses doctored for an auction.

The family stayed close working together even when the children had grown up and made their own families. Zillah remembered that when she was a child her family worked and travelled frequently with Granddad Albert and Granny Mary. To make a living her dad and granddad worked together grinding knives and scissors and Granddad Albert occasionally made shoes for customers with odd shaped feet. They also made pegs and baskets for Granny Mary and her mam to sell. She cast herself back to how her parents and grandparents used to go door-to-door selling to keep the family. It was hard in those days as there was no money. They only lived day to day.

She recalled how "some days we would have food and some days we wouldn't." Her dad, when Zillah was a child, would sometimes have to catch a rabbit or a hedgehog to make them a meal. They did all the cooking outside on a stick fire on tin trays or in an old black Gypsy pot. She didn't like watching her dad preparing and cooking a hedgehog, hated the taste of it and has refused to eat it all her life. "I watched 'im once or twice and didn't like it but it was because we were hungry and had to eat something. After killing the hotchi (hedgehog) with a dagger me dad held 'im by 'is back legs and stood on 'is front feet. Then Dad pulled 'im tight working with a sharp knife to shave the bristles downwards to 'is nose. Then he held 'im over the flames with the knife turning him gently around and over to singe off any bristle and hair that was left. The hotchi's back swelled up to almost double its size and the whole thing turned black and looked like a bowler hat. I couldna bear to watch but somehow Dad gutted it and threw away the gall bladder, washed it all out and cooked it in a tray on the fire like any other meat."

Despite the desperate experiences of hunger and poverty, Zillah remembered fondly the times spent with her grandparents after the food was eaten and the chores were done, her mam and the aunties step dancing[6] and yodelling around the fire to Irish jigs and Gypsy songs played on the fiddle by her father and the uncles on accordion and spoons.

She remembered how her granddad, her dad and the other men brewed their own beer and wine by drying nettles for days and boiling them with elderberries in a big black pot on the fire. They strained the liquid into stone jars and left it to mature for weeks before consumption. Her dad Albert, a great believer in herbal remedies "could make many remedies for painful swollen legs. Comfrey leaves were dipped in boiling water and laid on the swollen area. Comfrey was also good for headaches and when made into tea it was good for stomachache. Dock leaves was for stinging nettles and insect stings. There was a lot more but I can't remember what they was. I know he learnt them from his mam and dad."

Zillah's grandfather died aged just 60 years old when she was still small. Though Granny Mary lived on for a couple of years, she never stopped grieving for her husband. She decided to settle at Sound Common, near Nantwich in Cheshire. Zillah and her family always looked forward to going there twice a year to see her and the rest of the family.

Zillah remembered the family wending their way down the lanes to the Common and like the other chavs wanting to eat the red berries, called bread and cheese, in the bushes. She could still smell the scents of bluebell and lilac flowers as their varda brushed past and even then truly believed that God had made these sweet berries and scents for her and all Romany people.

In particular she remembered one night when she was walking away from Granny Mary's varda on Sound Common. "I saw a lady all in white and she looked as if she was floating. She was calling out, 'I want me brother Henry'. I was so scared I began to run to me mam and I fell in a hole and an old bike wheel stuck in my cheek. I was screaming so loud me dad and everybody else on the common came running. Me dad, uncles and aunties all saw the lady in white and me dad told me it was me Aunty Dolly, Granny Mary's sister, who died on the common. She always seemed to appear when all the family was on the common. I never saw anything like this before and me dad said, 'Don't be scared because the dead won't hurt you only the living. She is a guardian angel looking after all of us'."

Granny Mary died soon after that in 1930 aged 65 years when Zillah was 5 years old: old enough to remember Granny Mary's burning caravan and the family's guardian angel Auntie Dolly.

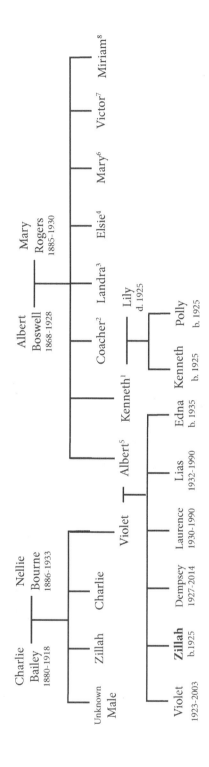

Picture 10: Bailey and Boswell family tree 1865 - 1935

Charlie
Bailey
1880-1918

Nellie
Bourne
1886-1933

Albert
Boswell
1868-1928

Mary
Rogers
1885-1930

Unknown
Male

Zillah

Charlie

Violet

Albert[5]

Kenneth[1]

Coacher[2]

Landra[3]

Elsie[4]

Mary[6]

Victor[7]

Miriam[8]

Lily
d. 1925

Violet
1923-2003

Zillah
b.1925

Dempsey
1927-2014

Laurence
1930-1990

Lias
1932-1990

Edna
b. 1935

Kenneth
b. 1925

Polly
b. 1925

Chapter 2

The arrival of Zillah (1900-1935)

"Who do wild things run for if not for those as wild as themselves?"

As Zillah looked at the pictures of her mam and dad, Violet and Albert, back in her newly refurbished trailer, not for the first time she was thankful for, and proud of, her good Romany family. They had gone to all this effort to surprise her after the birthday meal and she loved her brand new soft rugs, matching curtains and bone china figurines. She had new photos taken with her daughters and sons, and it was at times like these she remembered and missed her husband, parents and other dearly loved ones lost along the way. The older she grew, the more often she found herself reflecting back on her childhood and her loving parents.

Picture 11: Zillah, March 2015

Zillah's parents were both from North Staffordshire. Albert was a Romany Gypsy born in 1898 in Staffordshire with family from both Stoke-on-Trent and near Manchester. Zillah could still picture him as, "a tall dark man who always

Picture 12: Albert, Zillah's dad, with his Varda c.1922

weared a scarf round 'is neck, a handsome Gypsy man. He wasn't a talker and kept to 'imself. He was a strict dad but 'e never hit us and I used to sit on 'is lap." She loved listening to him playing the accordion, fiddle and mouth organ. Her favourite was "Take Me Home Again Kathleen" and it still makes her cry whenever she hears it.

Her mother Violet was a fair-haired Gorgia woman born in 1902 to a Gorgio family from Burslem. She had been working as a nurse in a hospital up there when she met and fell in love with a Gypsy man- Albert Boswell- back in 1921. They kept in touch and then ran away to jump the broomsticks on Sound Common. She was 18 years old and he was 23. The Boswells accepted Violet and her Bailey family including her siblings, Zillah's Uncle Charlie and her Aunt Zillah. Albert Senior made a varda for his son and new wife. Mary also gave them a bed, a quilt made by herself and some porcelain tea cups.

The Baileys accepted the marriage too apart from one brother who became estranged from Violet and her new family. "He hated Gypsies because his sister ran away with one. So he'd tell Gypsies at the door to 'go away because your people took my sister away'. I think me parents were shunned at the start with people saying, 'Dordi, Dordi, look at him he's got a Gorgie raki!' but me mam took to the Gypsy life and they took to her." Over the years she got to look more and more like a Gypsy despite her fair hair. Nearly all of her children were dark like their dad but Zillah took after her mam with very light blonde hair. Her Auntie Zillah called her "the white witch" much to everyone's amusement!

Zillah's maternal grandparents were Charlie Bailey, born in Staffordshire in about 1880 and Nellie Bourne, born in Birmingham in 1886. Neither of her maternal parents was from a Gypsy family and Zillah remembered how her mam's parents had owned a sweet shop in Stoke. One of her early memories, when she was four and her sister was six, is the horse drawn Reading Varda stopping on a piece of ground near Burslem not far from the shop. "There was a row of houses on the main road on top of Hanley. Granny's house was made into a shop and had one window full of jars of sweets. Everything smelt lovely with the old fashioned sweets – pear drops, jelly babies in white paper bags and humbugs. Granny was a big fat lady with a happy round kind face."

She never saw her mam's dad Charlie but she'd seen her mam's photo of him with all his medals. The photo has disappeared and Zillah thinks

it was probably put in the grave with him, as that was the custom. She was told that Granddad had been a colonel in the army and that he died when Zillah was just eight. Granny Nellie died soon after when Zillah was nine. Violet's brother Charlie went over to France in the war married a French woman and didn't come back though he did write to his family. Violet never went over to France to see him but she and her family stayed in touch with her sister Zillah for the rest of their lives.

Picture 13: Violet with her first baby Violet 1923

Thinking back it seemed to Zillah that Violet was so much in love with Albert that she was happy to travel the lanes with him and soon adapted to the Gypsy way of life. Maybe she was glad to leave behind the smoke and hard grind of living in Burslem. She often told Zillah how she had loved travelling with Albert and the family through the countryside around the Potteries and the flat plains of Cheshire. Violet soon became an important member of her new family. She was seen as a scholar and always had a book to hand. She read for them and wrote their letters as well as being a good listener when they had problems. The children and grandchildren thought she was lovely especially when she was in a good mood reaching behind the cushion on the seat of the varda for her bag of sweets to distribute amongst them. Sometimes, when not in a good mood, she'd say, " Go away you little Gypsy tinkers, shoo shoo!" but they knew she loved them.

The life of Zillah began on 20th March 1925 during the brief pause between the wars. She was born near Crab Lane on the northern edge of Stafford and was the second of six children that Violet would go on to have. Zillah's birth was fairly typical at that time for Romany families. Although the Midwives Act in England had been passed some twenty years previously, Romany families were largely unaware and unaffected by it. Romany families still relied upon their own "bone fide" midwives. They not only attended the birth and got the mother settled with her baby, but also cleaned up the caravan, and did the laundry. For another two shillings the midwife would come back for the next few days. The whole business of childbirth was strictly in the realm of mothers, grandmothers and midwives. Husbands and children were kept out of it.

Picture 14: Kenneth down Crab Lane, Stafford c1935

In the years immediately following Zillah's birth, Violet went on to have Dempsey and Lawrence and by 1930 was expecting another. Zillah grew up knowing nothing about how and where babies came from. Her mother and other family members never talked about it. Zillah would often recall the birth of her youngest brother Lias. Because Violet was expecting the family stayed for some time at Crab Lane in Stafford where her dad's brother Kenneth lived with his twin chavs Polly and Kenneth (aka Kensa). Everyone in that North end of Stafford and up to Stone knew him as he was a fortuneteller, horse dealer and collected scrap metal and rags. Being near a town with midwives and having Kenneth's support was important by the time Lias was due.

When the time came her dad Albert went on his horse and cart to fetch the midwife and when asked where he was going, he simply told the chavs, "Fetch some water. Put it there till I come back an' then go down that lane an' don't come back till we fetch you". So Zillah and her siblings sat on a stile down Crab Lane wondering what was the matter. There was an old barn where an old tramp would sometime lay. Zillah and the other children thought he was the mulla (devil) until their dad told them not to talk daft and said, "It's only a poor old tramp he won't hurt yer. He's got nowhere to go." But they were not thinking of him that day only what the worry was with dad. Soon they spotted, "a woman comin' with a case with a blue coat on an' a blue hat." It was about four o'clock, near dusk. In the distance they could make out their dad standing outside the varda, heating water in a big pot on a huge stick fire. Then he'd walk around and watch the grais (horses) .

When the midwife had gone and everything was all over Albert whistled for them to come back up. They knew that if they didn't go to him he'd come down looking for them and shout at them. They heard him and said to each other, "Did you hear him whistle? He's gonna kill us if we don't go back to the varda now."

They used to frighten each other walking along Crab Lane thinking there was somebody in the bushes when they heard all the little sticks cracking.

So it was they clung together in the gathering gloom as they returned to the varda. When they got back Albert whispered, "Come on now everythin' is alright. You've got a little brother an' we'll 'ave 'im named Lias." Zillah remembered how she and her siblings all wanted to know what had happened. Her father had explained to them that the nurse, "fetched yer little brother in the case." This satisfied them and later Zillah thought, "He is a lovely baby though."

Uncle Kenneth took Violet, Zillah's older sister, out on the cart to do her mam's shopping until after two weeks when she was "churched" and able to start going back out again. This was a kind of purification ritual practice for women after giving birth to avoid being mokadi (unclean). It is part of a strict code of cleanliness learnt over centuries of life on the road. Concepts such as mokadi place strict guidelines, for example, on what objects can be washed in what bowls. It involved Violet only preparing food for herself using her own cutlery, dishes and cups. Nowadays it is a ceremony practiced by some Gorgias in church and by all strict Gypsy women including the women in Zillah's family.

At around this time Zillah's mam taught her two daughters useful crafts. "She would learn us to knit, sew and crochet but we only liked crocheting. So we decided to crochet mam a patchwork blanket with all colours of wool that me mam had begged for. Vi and me sat for hours making squares and it took us months to make this blanket. Me mam was so proud of us. It was her favourite blanket and she showed it to all her friends."

Picture 15: The family's open lot varda with Albert, Lawrence, Lias and Violet

In those early years the family experienced some of the coldest winters for years and the economic depression of the interwar years was hitting them hard. Zillah's early childhood was marked by the seasons with winters being particularly hard. Zillah remembered those difficult times. "When Vi and I were little chavvies we used to stop up nice country lanes with our vardas and our daddy used to go out grinding knives and scissors to earn us some bread. He sharpened scissors, knives and lawnmower blades for householders and butchers using a grinding stone and a pedal to make it go. We'd always have to go and walk miles in the snow down the lanes to tie the grais (horses) up and find somewhere for the vardas for the family to stop for the day and night. He'd come back with 'is hands all frostbitten and the snow was up the varda steps. One day he came back with so much frost bite that he warmed his hands on a jumper, put olive oil on his fingers and then soaked them in warm water. Our mam used to make pegs out of straight willow sticks and when they'd been shaped and dried she'd go selling them with little Lias wrapped up to her in a Gypsy shawl."

They had an open lot varda with a curtain instead of a door in those days when there was just Zillah, Vi, Dempsey, Lawrence and baby Lias and their mam and dad. They slept on tick straw mattresses with a Welsh quilt cover. Albert and Violet slept in a double bed with baby Lias. Zillah and Violet slept together underneath in a little cupboard while Dempsey and Lawrence slept on the floor in the winter and under the varda in the summer. The stove kept them warm and it had an oven at the side with two rings for cooking. Their mam cooked rabbits, dumplings, ham and bacon bones and it could be smelt all down the lanes. As long as they had coal they all kept lovely and warm inside the varda. When they ran out though they had to go foraging for wood. Zillah never forgot those winters and she often still wondered how they survived.

The worst winter of her childhood days was when they were old enough to go to school. Zillah remembered how one snowy day she, Vi and Dempsey managed to get to the school all right but the snow, "came that heavy we couldna get back. We were up Crab Lane with the snow right up to the top of the hedge and it was burying us chavs as we was going along. We was frightened to death crying. The varda that'd come to fetch us couldn't get through because it was stuck on top of another lane, Lion's Den." Not knowing if help was on its way they just cried for their mam and dad and huddled together. Eventually Albert did come and dug his way down to them from the top of the lane to get them home.

Apart from the cold winters with snow piling up against the varda door and some hungry days Zillah and her sister and brothers were only vaguely aware of their parent's worries. Life for them during these interwar years and before they were school age was much the same as it had always been for Travelling children - like it had been for their father, and his siblings. They felt as free as birds, playing and working during the day either with their dad Albert and the other grown-ups at the camp or going hawking with their mam Violet and the other women.

Summers brought the easiest times although sometimes the vardas got very hot and the tarmac melted. They had no pantry so keeping food fresh was a problem. The bread went as hard as a stone and they kept the milk and butter in water to stay cool.

During these warmer months the family along with Uncle Kenneth and his chavs moved on to Beaconside in Stafford. "Passers-by would stop and ask if they could come and have a look at our Gypsy caravans so me dad would show them. Inside it was pretty and me dad was so proud of it." Her dad turned his horses out in the field behind the varda and his cart would be at the side.

Zillah remembered Beaconside as a lovely place with a wood and running spring where they could play. She remembered the gorse bushes like "little trees in a circle with all green leaves and little yellow bacon and egg flowers". She and the other chavvies used to make a little house in the circle and get their pots and pans and play. She had lovely memories of playing all day making chains of buttercups and daisies while listening to the birds singing. They played skipping and hopscotch or made a swing in a tree. They were never bored and enjoyed every minute. In the warm summer months the days seemed like they were never going to end as they walked along the lanes looking in the hedges for birds' eggs and hedgehogs while picking bluebells and wild flowers for their mam. "Our mams would be out selling pegs and flowers and our dads gone out with the grais and carts scrapping iron."

In the evenings their mam "allus made the tea and we would be sitting on the grass and my mother would put a table and a white cloth on the grass and put a pot on it with rabbit broth or cabbage and potatoes. At night we would listen to me dad playing 'is fiddle and me uncles playing their spoons and all the ladies step dancing on the board. They really enjoyed their music on the commons with the sounds of it ringing through the air and the villagers loving to hear it." The Gorgias passing by also liked to watch her dad making baskets with willow sticks and flowers from elder twigs that would take him hours to finish. Meanwhile Zillah, Vi and Polly, their cousin, stood barefoot in the spring washing their clothes with an old scrubbing board and mangle.

Later in the evening "Mam would wash all of us outside and put us to bed. There were only two beds in the varda so the girls slept in one and my mam and dad had the other one. Me brothers slept on the floor of the varda. I remember we were woke up by the singing of the birds. This was our alarm clock. Me dad 'ad a fire going and we would 'ave a wash and dad would make us toast and then we went to play and mam walked miles to the nearest village to sell her pegs and baskets and beg for clothes and shoes as we never 'ad any money to buy them. What bit of money we made in the summer had to be saved for the winter as I remember. Many a time we'd nothin' to eat only the berries on the trees."

Depending on the weather, sometimes the chavs would go out and sometimes they wouldn't. If it was raining they would watch the raindrops on the varda window. If the drops didn't run one into the other they knew there'd be fine weather coming. On those rainy days they played eye-spy, one potato two potato and threaded beads to practice counting.

One of Zillah's abiding memories of her childhood was having to walk for miles to earn a living. They travelled mainly along country roads through villages. Zillah had fond memories of stopping on an aerodrome where planes used to land. This was Cheetham Hill near Manchester where they travelled on the trams with their mam to visit Auntie Zillah, her mam's Gorgia sister. Their dad's brothers would join them all back at the camp and sit around the fire making pegs, baskets and flowers for their wives to sell.

Sometimes they travelled as far down as Swansea in Wales. But mostly they travelled around Stafford and the Potteries. In the summer they headed south for the fruit and hop picking via Stafford, camping on Milford Common, then on to Lichfield and down to Evesham. They'd have to stop frequently at different places because of the grais and vardas. Everyday was the same; minding the grais, cleaning the vardas, making a living, moving from one place to another. The gavvers used to move them on but in Zillah's experience they were more lenient in those days. When Gypsy families were miles down a lane and there were only a few of them the gavvers would often let them stop and give them to the next day to move on.

However, many farmers wanted Gypsies off their land there and then and whether it was night or day they had to hitch up the horse to the varda and find somewhere else to pull in. It used to be hard when they couldn't stop long and had to find another place. Sometimes they got shouted at, or worse threatened with a stick and calling the gavvers, for putting their horses in a farmer's field. They couldn't bear to see the grais go hungry and Gypsies saw no harm in putting them to graze on private land. The way Zillah's family saw it, "grass was growing there before ever a farmer lived and the Lord didn't put it there for any one person. And one day the Lord's grass will be growing over us all amongst the poppies and buttercups." If one of their jukkels (dogs) happened to come to the varda with a rabbit in its mouth they'd be thrown off for poaching. But the way Zillah saw it, "they'd be throwing the Lord's good work in His face not to eat it. Who do wild things run for if not for those as wild as themselves?"

Her dad went grinding knives to save money for the hay and straw and shoeing the grais that he "looked after as if they were his chavs". One time Zillah remembered how their grai had a disease of the feet and they had to have her put down. Her feet were bleeding all the time and they used to have her walking on the grass. Albert would pull the wagon himself before he'd let her suffer. He got in the shafts of the varda and pulled it himself with some of the chavs pushing it from the back. They were very hard times and they never had any money to buy another grai. But however hard her early family life was, her parents always made sure they lived a good life as "proper Romanies."

This did not mean always having to be on the move. In fact, Zillah's family didn't want to travel continuously and of course they didn't like to be moved on forcibly. They had their favourite places and it was really good to stay settled in one place like Sound Common near Nantwich for a while. There were always two or three vardas together and they formed a rough circle to make an encampment.

They always found a spring and carried the water from it to do their washing in a big black pot. They knew where the springs were wherever they went and could hear them running. They only had to scrape a little hole if the stream was a good one. Her dad was very good at finding the streams. He used to go along the lanes and listen for the dribbling of the water. Sometimes they'd be in little lanes around Armitage or in

a field or on a common like at Milford. As soon as he'd heard a little drop he'd scrape a big hole with a shovel and "then it would all come and us chavs would wait until it was flowing out into this big hole, which was like a trench or a bath big enough to put a bucket in".

Picture 16: Gypsy Horse Mare.(Mary E. Graybeal).

24

Her dad loved Stafford. It was on the circuit between his mother's people, the Rogers and Violet's folk, the Baileys, both up in Stoke. They'd travel around with about ten vardas or sometimes four and meet up with the others later if they stayed on in Stafford down Crab Lane or up on Milford Common. If they lost one another they put grass or sticks in the shape of arrows along the old-fashioned signposts to show which way they were going.

Despite all the movings on Zillah remembers a time when they felt relatively safe as they moved around the countryside. They mostly lived harmoniously alongside the Gorgias. Her uncle Kenneth and his twin girls, Polly and Kensa, were always with Zillah's family in those early days as their mam had died a few weeks after they were born. Ladies had their fortunes told by Uncle Kenneth by palm and face reading and in exchange would give him frocks for his daughter Polly. Zillah remembered how jealous she was of these dresses and how she wanted them for herself. Zillah thinks that the twins did all right living with them and that Polly and Kensa turned out well despite losing their mam and despite the second war.

The years between the wars passed down the lanes in the usual Gypsy style. When Zillah was ten years old everyone Gorgia and Gypsy alike was preparing celebrations for the Silver Jubilee of King George V and Queen Mary. Zillah's dad washed and brushed his grai, "until it shone like a glass bottle". He cleaned the harness and all the brasses and then plaited the grai's tail with blue and white ribbons. Like all the other roms he decorated the harness with ribbons, cleaned the cart and took his grai into town where most of the horse dealing would be done on that Jubilee day.

Back at the camp the men played horseshoes throwing them over a steel bar stuck in the ground. The first to get five horseshoes over was the winner. Afterwards around the fire at night there was singing and dancing and the telling of tales from long ago. However, on this day Albert and the other Gypsies were more concerned about recent events. They were becoming aware of trouble brewing in the Gorgio world. By 1935 stories of persecution of Gypsies and Jews were reaching them from across the Channel.

In the meantime life continued and when Zillah's mam had their last child, Edna, she was still trying to persuade Zillah now 10 years old to learn to read. But for Zillah being taught to read was like having

Picture 17 : Lias with his jukkel c.1942

someone "blowing in her ears". Zillah has never learnt to read even though her mother could.

Zillah remembered that they were staying at Sound Common the first time she and Violet went to school. She and her siblings never liked school much. Zillah always remembered how the teacher would say to her, "Spell that, it says 'basket.'" But Zillah couldn't spell it and the teacher would make her say it over and over again. "Me mam tried to teach me to read many a time saying, 'cat an' dog' and all that sort of caper but I never had the patience. "

The attitudes of the Gorgio children in school didn't help either. Zillah was very bright but she was determined never again to go to school, "after those Gorgio children kept chingerin' (fighting) me saying, 'Oh look at the dirty gippo' and hittin' Dempsey when he called them names back. I told him to take no notice but he didn't listen and I just carried on chingerin' back meself."

Her way of dealing with the Gorgio insults was to laugh at their scruffy clothes, dirty faces and tangled hair and say, "Look at yourself! Yer hair 'asn't been combed out this mornin'- it's all tatty an' never bin combed for a week! It's all messed up and dirty", and, "We're cleaner than you lot! "(Violet was a very proud and fussy mother).

Of course that made the Gorgios even madder at both her and at Dempsey so they spent much of their time at school hiding. Although she did over time have Gorgio friends, she was so set against school that, by the time she was ten, she couldn't even bear to look at the letters in her mother's books. Zillah preferred the freedom that being a Gypsy gave her.

They never bought anything in the way of clothes. They had what people gave them and never had to worry about losing anything. They

26

could leave their varda and everything in it and it'd still be all right. The chavs were free to go miles down lanes and they never got hurt. They'd walk miles over fields to get to the shops for their dad's fags. They were never frightened and they could always go there and back in peace. Zillah enjoyed running and jumping over the stiles, picking buttercups and making daisy chains. Then they'd get the fags and come back and Dad would say, "Where've you bin' all this time!"

But it was different in those days. Now snug in her "made over" trailer and entering her 91st year with Grace and John, young Abigail, Nathan and her other great grandchildren beside her she thought to herself that despite their chirpiness, their little phones and game gadgets in this world today the children's lives are not their own.

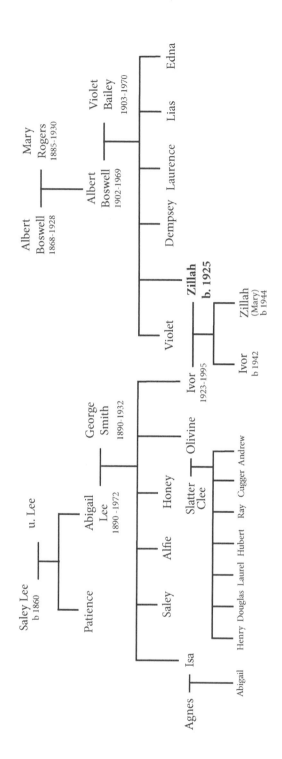

Picture 18 Lee, Boswell and Smith Family Tree 1860-1945

Chapter 3

Zillah makes her own life 1935-1945

"I was born in a ditch, that's why I'll never grow rich"

Picture 19: Zillah in her trailer at Glover Street January 2015

Two months before her 90th birthday Zillah had been confined to her trailer with a chest infection so her days were spent in bed in the mornings and receiving visits from her sons and daughters and their families in the afternoons and evenings.

It just so happened that on 27th January 2015 Zillah, still in her pyjamas, switched on the TV at about midday after rising from her cosy bed.

It was Holocaust Memorial Day and someone on the TV was saying that it was the 70th anniversary of the liberation of Auschwitz. Events were being held all over the world.

One of the most striking of these was the reading out loud continuously of the names of those killed in the holocaust but who had no marked graves. Carried out by a relay of 700 people over a continuous 112 hour period, the event took place at the former transit camp at Westerbork in the north of the Netherlands. The whole event could be followed on a live stream of the Dutch television and now Zillah saw a short clip and the commentator said that some of names belonged to Gypsies.

Then another item followed about a place called Calais. Refugees were living in a camp and she saw what it was like. Up until then she wasn't very clear in her head about what her opinion was about refugees. Grace and John had told her off on more than one occasion when she used to say there were too many foreigners coming into the country.

Now seeing pictures of the camp and the people in it she was beginning to agree with her son and daughter that it wasn't that different from the way Gypsies were treated in the war and are still treated and talked about now. In fact she felt hot with the anger rising within and tears filling her eyes as she remembered the plight of her own mother one of those desperate days in her childhood. The family was so hungry one winter with nothing to eat and no money that her mother got a note from a kind policeman giving her permission to beg for food for her to take around the houses.

Zillah heated up some soup, toasted a pikelet and turned down the volume on the TV as all this had started her off thinking and remembering. Zillah's childhood had disappeared during her teenage years with the threat of another war looming. She was 14 years old when the Second World War broke out, and aged just 16 when she got married 2 years later. By the end of the war she was a mother of two small children, Ivor and Mary. Her marriage was the usual story of an elopement like that of her mother and father. Ivor was Zillah's first and only boyfriend. Parents wouldn't let their children court anybody in those days. Gypsy teenagers had to court secretly and they "daren't tell their mam and dad because they'd get a good hiding." As far as their parents were concerned young teenagers were still chavvies until they were in their late teens. Albert, Violet and other Gypsy parents were strictly protective of their girls.

Picture 20: Zillah c.1939

Despite this Zillah still found a way to go to the pictures with her Gypsy Romany friends. Sometimes the boys as well as the girls used to be there but when she used to court Ivor she went on her own. She had known him years before when they were chavs pulling up together in Longton and other places. Then after a long time she met him again when she was fourteen. By this time, Vi, her sister, was courting his brother Saley Smith and when they got married Zillah started courting Ivor. They were all stopping at Brownhills in a field behind the Fighting Cocks Farm and Ivor would come over to her varda with Saley.

Ivor was eighteen years old and "a real kushti mush as dark as a Gitano[7] from Spain". He held his whole body straight and his head high just like a Spanish dancer. His hair was glossy black and brushed back so his forehead looked high with a bit of a widow's peak.

Zillah thought he was really handsome with big dark eyes. To her he looked like a film star and all her friends were jealous. "He had a little curl to 'is lips that made it look like he was laughing at sommat, or pr'aps it was his shiny black eyes that gave him that jokey look. He liked to look smart with 'is shirts dark coloured, usually black with white down the collar and a bright red neckerchief or a white tie when he really got dressed up. He had a blue serge suit, tailor-made when he - or his mam - could afford it."

They went out secretly for a while and Zillah often chuckled at the memory of Ivor coming to her parent's varda and asking permission to go out with her even though she had already been going out with him for some time. Ivor asked her to marry him in 1940 and she said,

"I don't know - me dad'll kill me!" He replied, "Well, we'll run away an' they won't know nothin'!" So they planned to get married on the sly without telling anyone. They were stopping at Muckley Corner in South Staffordshire at the time and when they went to the pictures in Walsall they put their name down at the local registry office.

The wedding was booked for the 27th March a week after her 16th birthday. When it was time they simply went on a bus to Walsall town and asked a Gorgio couple on the street outside the registry office to be their witnesses.

Zillah remembered the couple well, the woman in particular. She took a liking to the two youngsters and thought they were a very handsome couple. She told Zillah that she looked a beauty with her golden wavy hair and blue eyes. Zillah had never thought of herself as beautiful before then but that day she felt it. Ivor's eyes were shining even more than before and he had such a big smile on his face she couldn't help but laugh and so did the woman, their witness. The woman crossed their palms with silver as a wedding gift and Zillah has kept that half a crown to this day and will never part with it.

Picture 21 Portrait painted of Zillah and Ivor c.1940

After the wedding they bought a 9 by 9 foot tent and went off on their own for a couple of nights and went back to their families "as fresh as a pair of newly picked daffs." Ivor went and told his mam and then Albert and Violet who said, "If you're married you've made your bed. You got to lay on it." It was what Zillah wanted and she never regretted it.

She had married into the Smith family but was also a Lee because of Ivor's maternal family from Wales. She remembered fondly how he could still speak a bit of Welsh jib (language) in his old age and pictured their last old Reading varda that Ivor's brother made for them still over in Wales.

During the war life was hard and stressful for the young newly weds. In many ways their way of living was much the same for them as it had been for her parents when Vi and Zillah were chavs. They'd go from one lane to another gravitating to commons, like Milford, Pipehill and Pelsall and always calling into the Fighting Cock's field on the way to Walsall. With the war however, things were scarce and they had nothing apart from what the family gave them such as tablecloths, teapots and whatever else that could be spared.

Zillah's parents grew to really like Ivor and thought the world of him. Their two daughters had married two brothers, and Violet could see that though a bit wild in their feelings both men could control their tempers. Zillah agreed and told her mam that Ivor always said after he married her, "If I ever get upset I don't want to hit yer, but don't keep on at me because I'll lose me temper. Before I hit you I'll hit summat else." So he'd hit a cupboard or he'd throw a plate outside. "Or I'll walk away", he said, "but don't say nothin' to me when I'm upset."

As far as Zillah was concerned "all of that kind of thing happened in life and it wouldn't be life if it didn't. Travellers have their off days. There's got to be a row in family life or it wouldn't be life would it? Sometimes Gypsy men if they got upset they'd have a fight and challenge one another out. They'd fight bare fisted but after one had beat the other everything would be all right. They'd quarrel over grais or if anyone said anything about their romni." Zillah remembered proudly that if any Gypsy upset her dad and he'd not done anything to deserve it he'd definitely have a fight bare fists. He wouldn't have anybody push him around. She also remembered that her mam had a temper sometimes but "she wasn't one for rowing. She'd just tell people what she thought but she'd never hit anybody."

Ivor had a wild temper and when he was upset he came out with his Welsh Romany jib. His dad, mam, granny and great granny were Welsh and all spoke Welsh. His family the Lees and Smiths came from Welshpool. Ivor spent his childhood in Wales where his dad George Smith met his mother Abigail Lee. Ivor and his brother Isa made baskets to sell and looked after the grais for his granddad and his great granddad – the famous Saley Lee well known around Welshpool for his flowers and pegs.

Picture 22: George Smith, Ivor's dad c.1930

In their younger days, Ivor and Isa would ride a lot of wild grais on the big commons after catching and breaking them in. Most of his family was now dead including his sister Olivine but some of his other relations were still living in Wales. Ivor's dad George died aged 42 when he was a boy and Abigail his mother brought up her five children on her own.

When Ivor married Zillah Abigail joined up with them. Abigail was a "dark haired Lee from Wales, a very smart and beautiful woman with a tiny waist, thick wavy hair and dark with a flower above her ear. She kept her age well till she was 80 odd or more." She was very well liked and had a reputation as a very good fortuneteller. She and George had 5 children some being dark and some fair haired. They were Olivine, Honey, Iza, Alfie, Ivor and Saley. She was good at cooking rabbits and hedgehogs around a stick fire for her grandchildren who also loved her Gypsy cakes and bacon puddings. Later when she was very old, the local policeman "was allus bringin' 'er back 'ome tellin' 'er she was too old to go out sellin' from 'er basket" and eventually died at Rickerscote in her varda soon after Zillah's own parents in the 1970s. She was in her 80s and had lost Alfie and Iza before she died. After her funeral her remaining sons, Saley and Ivor, burnt her varda to the ground at Rickerscote while all the family including Zillah watched.

Picture 23: Laurel, Abigail Smith, Abi, Agnes Smith c.1940

During their teenage years when Zillah was just 17 and Ivor was 19, they began the wartime struggle of beginning to raise a family in 1941. Zillah knew little of what to expect apart from what her sister Vi used to tease her about when they were girls. She remembered how they would giggle together about getting married. Vi would say to her, "Ooh you got a lot to go through!" and Zillah would answer back, "Oh well never mind-I'll 'ave to go through it". She certainly did, bearing 13 children of her own, becoming a grandmother 61 times over, becoming a great grandmother 194 times over. At the last count she had 40 great great grandchildren. Her daughter Grace still teases Zillah about how she and Ivor together helped populate the world with at least an additional 308 people. Little did young Zillah know then what her fortune held for her.

Picture 24: Ivor, Zillah's first child, c.1942

Ivor was not called up to fight in the war "due to him not being A1", and a year after they were married her first son was born and according to tradition was named after his father, Ivor. Her next child, Zillah Mary, was traditionally named after her mother but always went by her second name. Ivor was born in a biggish round green bender with a pointed top. Normally they put down the floorboards, then the top with the hooks to hang curtains round to cover the tent poles. However, as it was the war they couldn't get curtains to put around the sides. The tent was round like a wigwam with a hole for a chimney. For the newly wed Zillah it was "very nice and comfortable with chairs an' tables on' a wooden floor with a nice old-fashioned Queen Anne Stove in the middle." When they moved it was all packed up on a flat dray (cart) and pulled along by the grai.

Picture 25: A Gypsy Encampment with bender early 20th century

It was in that bender that Zillah suffered with scarletina when Ivor was just five months old. At first it was just a little rash and her mam pound up elder for the pith to make an ointment. But eventually they had to call a doctor. "It was in the winter and they stove the place out to kill all the germs where I'd been sleeping." Zillah was kept in isolation and Zillah remembered how when all her skin peeled off the doctor comforted her by saying, "You'll be like you was fifteen again. You'll have all new skin."

By the time Zillah had her second child, Mary, Gypsy women were expected to go into hospital alongside the Gorgias. By this time they were living in their horse drawn Reading varda at Neachell's Lane in between Bilston and Willenhall. When the time came, Zillah went to a hospital the other side of Walsall. She found it a terrible experience. "We new mothers and our babies were stuck in there unable to come out or do anything. Soldiers surrounded us in case the Germans were coming."

They heard aeroplanes flying over the hospital that used to be in darkness. But at least her husband, Ivor, was able to visit her while her sister Vi looked after young Ivor. There were also some enjoyable times. Zillah still remembered how one night all the women in her ward wanted some fish and chips. "A soldier went and got some and handed them through the window - oh we really enjoyed those fish and chips!" Zillah also "got on lovely with the women there". They all said how pretty Mary was exclaiming, "What a lovely little black haired baby! She's a proper little Gypsy girl!" And of course they kept asking Zillah to tell their fortunes.

Picture 26: Zillah and Mary 1943

As with the births of all her children Zillah stayed in bed for two weeks and did not prepare food, cook or visit anyone's home. This time she was "churched" when she left the hospital and got back into scraping a living as the war continued. Life had become even harder with very little available to sell from door to door. They now had to make wooden rather than paper flowers even though they couldn't rely so much on foraging for wood for fear of being caught up with the soldiers who were billeted there in the woods.

They managed though and Zillah hawked her wooden flowers carrying little Mary around her neck wrapped in a big red Welsh shawl. Other mothers would often ask her, "You allus carry your baby neat don't you? How do you keep your baby level like that?" She would explain that, "You wrap the chavvie in the sheet sling then you wrap the shawl around her and then you wrap the shawl around you and tuck it under. Then you have both hands free so you can carry things in both hands." Zillah was proud of the fact that she had perfected the wrapping technique so that Mary was always in the same place where she put her.

As well as the shortages of food and the difficulties of earning a living there was the ever-present anxiety and fear of being invaded. She remembered what an upsetting time it was. "It was all we could talk about an' there was a lot o' worry. We'd heard about what old Hitler was doin' to our people an' we was worried about what would 'appen if the Nazis come over 'ere. We'd heard that Hitler used to get all the chavs in a row an' shoot them down an' torture 'em. We couldn't read about it but we heard all that one an' another told us. There's a lot o' Gypsies walkin' around now who don't know they are Gypsies. Their parents in the war gave up the Gypsy life and pretended to be Gorgios in case Hitler won the war. They didn't tell their chavs that they were Gypsies."

Zillah often remembered how one time she was up in Wales with Ivor's family and they were sitting outside their old Reading varda having their tea. "Along came this rawni(woman) Gorgi - well she was

Picture 27: Zillah demonstrating the Welsh shawl with Miselli's grandson and granddaughter c.1990s

dressed like a Gorgi and spoke like one but when I looked into her face I could see she was Romani. She didn't know it though. Well when she sat down on the little seat opposite the Queen Anne Stove she just burst into tears and cried out, 'I was born in a caravan like this and I didn't know it till now!'"

"Yes", thought Zillah. "We lost a lot o' Gypsies in the last war out o' fear o' Hitler comin' over."

Memories kept flooding back for Zillah as she switched on the fire and sat enjoying the warmth of her trailer. During the war they couldn't have either lights or fires after dark.

They could have a fire in the varda but they couldn't have a big stick fire outside. They'd sometimes have a Tilley Lamp or a candle, which they'd blow out "When old Hitler was coming all over us dropping bombs. First we'd hear all the 'planes and we could tell when the Germans were over by the sound of 'em. We knew they weren't English so we'd get out of our vardas and run to the air raid shelter or a big ditch."

One night they were stuck in a shelter for four or five hours. "Loads more people were there, Gorgios as well, all on the floor or on big long seats cuddling together to keep warm. There'd be a crib to put Mary in and if the gas came we had gas masks ready on our backs." Another time before she was married they were camped up a lane near Brownhills having left the caravans and were running for the nearest shelter across the common. Bombs seemed to be falling the in the fields alongside them and Zillah remembered how "Me dad catched hold of us all and said, 'Duck!' and pushed us into a big ditch. It was big enough to stand in. We'd took a blanket to wrap round us until the all clear went. We were frightened to death. You could hear the bang and see the orange flare but we missed that thank the Lord."

With Zillah's own young family and the bombs still falling, they still celebrated Christmas as much as they could. Zillah used to make Ivor and Mary a little stocking each out of her nylons for them to hang up. She remembered putting an orange, an apple and a few nuts, some dolly mixtures, those little sweet cigarettes, or cigars with cream in the middle. They used to really enjoy it when it was quiet with no raids. "All the family'd be there an' we'd have a sing an' a dance. We'd have a bit o' fire but only in the daytime but if we heard an air raid come on we'd douse it straight away. We couldn't even light a fag then you know."

Every day life continued much the same living from hand to mouth. They'd have their rations and if they had enough coupons they might have a chicken or catch a rabbit, hare or pheasant with the jukkels catching them. Her dad was still good at catching a few rabbits and hedgehogs himself which also provided them with extra food. She remembered how her dad would stand on the back of a hedgehog and its head would come out. When the heads are in you can't kill 'em. He'd

hit it on the head with a stick and kill it. Quick death. It wouldn't be punished. Just one crack."

When the war ended Zillah was a 20-year-old wife and mother. Zillah remembered Victory Night when all the Gypsies got together on Muckley Common near the Old Boat Inn. They celebrated all night and were hopeful of a better life. Albert played the fiddle and his son Dempsey the accordion.

They put down a wooden board and Zillah and others step danced

Picture 28: Dempsey c.1945

and yodelled. The singing and dancing continued for hours and the fire lasted till morning. The chavs fell asleep and their parents and older siblings exchanged stories of the war. Zillah's family had lost a lot of their relations during the war either fighting abroad or from the bombing raids. Zillah's mam's sister Auntie Zillah talked about her time in the Women's Royal Army Corps.

Zillah still has a photo of her namesake in her WRAC uniform. She thought fondly how her auntie had always had a soft spot for uniforms, which was probably one reason she'd married a policeman before the war. They talked about her mother's brother Uncle Charlie and his wife from France too who were alive though they didn't know their whereabouts. One of the traditional Romany songs that Zillah remembered from that evening was The Romani Rai (Gentleman)[8] It was often sung and she could still remember the words:

I'm the Romani rai,
I'm a true didikai (rough Traveller),
I build all my castles beneath the blue sky,
I live in a tent and I don't pay no rent,
And that's why they call me... the Romani rai.
Kakka chavvie, dick (look) akai (there),
Father's gone to sell a mush a kushti grai,
And that's why they call him... the Romani rai.
I'm the Romani rai,
Just an old didikai,
My home is a mansion beneath the blue sky,
I was born in a ditch, that's why I'll never grow rich,
And that's why they call me... the Romani rai.

Zillah could see how the Gypsy lifestyle described in that song was already beginning to disappear in the years following the war. These post war years would prove to be the most influential part of Zillah's life as she matured and nurtured her growing family, establishing herself as a true Romany woman in these times of great social change.

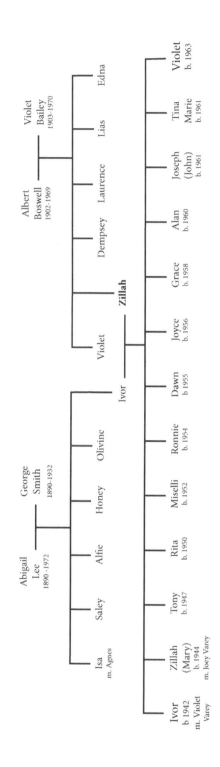

Picture 29 Smith Family Tree 1945-1963

Chapter 4

Zillah raises her young family 1945-1960

"It was so cold you'd think nobody could survive. But we did."

Picture 30: Grace and Zillah 2015

It was New Year's day 2015 and nearly three months before Zillah's ninetieth birthday. Her daughter Grace had come to stay with her for a few days after Christmas. She wanted to take her mother to the doctors as she was having trouble with the cold weather catching her breath and having dizzy turns. To cheer Zillah up Grace had brought her granddaughter Abigail who had three pieces of writing to read to her great granny. Two pieces were about her life as a Gypsy with drawings and the other was a poem. It ended in a way that Zillah liked - looking on the bright side.

"Relaxing on the grass, under the cool blue sky,
Whistling with the birds from way up high
Gypsies live with nature."

Abigail Birch Age 11. December 2014
(See Appendix 3 for the full poem)

Her poem and other writings expressed a love of her life as a Gypsy girl living on her family's small field on the edge of Temple Grafton a village near Stratford upon Avon. Zillah was pleased that her great granddaughter loved living close to nature, enjoyed her friendships at the village school, went to all the clubs and was learning the violin. Abigail's writing clearly showed her enthusiasm for her Gypsy life and also being part of life in an English Gorgia village. (Appendix 4)

Zillah was also relieved to hear that her great granddaughter's experience of school was very different from how it had been in her day. The poem reminded Zillah of her daughter Grace when she was a child as well as of her own childhood days of freedom.

Later that day, after Grace and Abigail had left to go up to Hopton to visit Zillah's other children John and Alan, Zillah was glad for some peace and quiet and a chance to think back to those days when her children were still young. In the post war years, those days were hard but it was still possible then to roam freely through the countryside and enjoy nature like young Abigail was able to now albeit on their little patch of land in Temple Grafton.

In those early days after the war ended Zillah's young family went up and down the lanes all over Staffordshire and beyond. They travelled around Lichfield, Pipehill, Pelsall Common, Neachell's Lane, Willenhall, Bilston and Walsall Wood.

It was a hard life as she and Ivor had more chavvies but they managed to bring all thirteen of them up in the Gypsy life. After Ivor and Mary, Zillah gave birth at one or two year intervals to: Tony, Rita, Miselli, Ronnie, Dawn, Joyce, Grace, Alan, and then the twins, John and Tina Marie in 1961. Her youngest child Violet was born in 1966 when Zillah was 38 years old. The eldest was born in a tent and the second in a hospital but the rest were born in horse drawn vardas and later trailers, except for the youngest three who were born in hospital.

It wasn't easy managing with so many babies and young children in the close confines of a varda but Zillah did it. She thought it was easy and best to feed them herself each for over a year. To her mind you didn't get pregnant when your breastfeeding. That's how it worked for her anyway. For nappies, she used proper napkins and sometimes she made them out of old thin blankets and bits of sheets. She remembered how the women did all that. "The men wasn't used to baby changing and we didn't like them to do anything like that. We always liked to look after the chavs ourselves. The men'd mind them or take them down the lanes to look at the grais but it was we women and the chavs who used to have to look after the grais watering and feeding them."

With the ordinary towelling napkins there was a lot of washing. After going to bed after midnight, Zillah typically got up at 5 'clock every morning to do the washing before the family got up. In winter the elders could hear her breaking the ice in the water so she could do the washing. "I'd take a bucket of cold water and me 'ands would be freezing till I couldn't feel them as I rubbed the nappies."

"We used to get the bucket o' water an' we'd slosh the nappy up an' down till all the stuff come off an' give it a little rub an' then put 'em in some Lux flakes. Put 'em in another big bucket an' soak 'em. Then they'd go in a big black pot, not the same as the cookin' pot. We used to boil 'em in that. I'd do that every day. I'd swill 'em in the mornin' an' when I come 'ome from hawkin', sellin' flowers, with the chavs, I'd pull the chavvie off me neck. Put the chavvie down, feed her meself, get me tea, give me other chavs their tea, an' then me 'usband went out to make some more flowers, an' I washed up an' then I did me napkins."

The main problem was drying them on the line she'd strung up. Sometimes when they were half dry she finished them off in the varda and ripped up an old sheet to use as napkins in the meantime. As they got older she used to say to them, "tell me when you want a wee" and she'd show them what to do. "If it was too bad weather I'd hold them over a pot to keep 'em out the cold. They was allus clean chavs an' knew what to do. When we were on the road we'd go behind hedges where nobody could see but when we were camped Ivor'd dig a hole and we'd gradually fill it in with earth. We'd put a tent around it." Zillah thought that was more natural and caused less damage than these modern flush toilets even though she was very grateful for the one she had in the trailer that John and her other sons and provided for her in her old age.

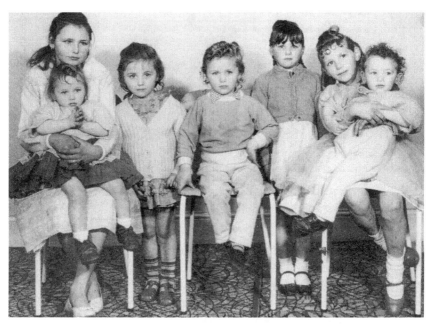

Picture 32: Miselli, Tina Marie, Grace, Alan, Joyce, Dawn, and John c.1962

Her gas fire gave out just enough heat but the calor gas was dear so life could still be cold in her trailer even nowadays. However, it was much harder when she was bringing up her chavvies. This was especially so during the cold season and Zillah remembered the infamous winter of 1947. She knew it was going to be bad as there were so many haws on the hedges. They called it the Big Snow. It wasn't as bad as the time she and her siblings got buried in snow when she was a child but people did suffer hard that winter of 1947. "It was so cold you'd think nobody could survive. But we did."

She knew because she'd witnessed it and so did Ivor and their three little chavs Ivor, Mary and baby Tony and their poor grai an' jukkel. Thankfully Ivor and his brother had built them a new open lot varda and they all had dry noses and a stove to keep them warm.

Grace had turned on the fire before they left and Zillah was now feeling warmer in her trailer. There were a few very early daffodils on the table that Grace and Abigail had brought. They reminded her of how much she and her family anticipated and welcomed Spring when it arrived. It was always a hopeful time and with the milder weather came more opportunities for eking out a living on the roads. By the time Spring came the frogs were spawning, the snowdrops and daffs had sprung up and they knew Summer was on its way. They'd make loads of pegs, wooden and paper flowers, and tins to sell. She remembered one year when the grai had given birth to a lovely brown foal and before long how she was big enough to pull the cart alongside her mammy who'd pull the new varda - they could be on their way.

They'd bought the new open lot varda with a bow roof from Ivor's brother Saley who was nearly always with them. Later they had a square Reading varda again made by Saley. Zillah thought of Ivor's sister, Olivine who had a son, Hubert Clee, who still makes old vardas. Zillah was proud that, unlike some Gypsies, her family used to make their own vardas and liked the idea that Hubert was keeping up the tradition. In her younger days they lined them out and carved wooden lions, horses and greyhound heads on the front with gilt and many different colours. "When we all moved on together the vardas were so beautiful all shining and hand painted. All the villagers looked at us as we passed their houses. At the back of the varda there was a kettle boy and all the black pots and pans would be hangin' and all us chavvies would be walkin' on the grass verge as the vardas went along. The scent of the tress, blossom and lilac was a pleasure to smell."

Zillah rummaged in a drawer and hooked out an old black and white photograph of a young girl hand on hip, standing at the top of the steps of an ornately carved and painted caravan. The girl's right high heeled foot was pointing forwards as if to start dancing and her right hand rested lightly on the closed bottom half of the door into her home. Through the open top half was a glimpse of light shining through a snowy white curtain and illuminating the interior of the caravan. It was her older sister Violet standing on Zillah's first Reading varda.

The young Violet, caught in time, was gazing out confidently from the photograph.

Despite the sepia of the photograph Zillah could imagine the rich red of the silken shawl. The woman's skirt looked to be of the same colour and had a filmy texture. A long white necklace sparkled. In her old age Zillah missed Vi. They had both told fortunes and were considered to have had the gift. They were both able to read the faces of people.

Although she and Vi had the same shape face her hair was different from Zillah's strawberry blonde curls. Violet's was long, thick, wavy and dark often a flower above her ear. The sisters had lived all their childhood and teenage years in vardas pulled by grais.

Picture 33: Violet, Zillah's older sister, on Zillah and Ivor's Reading Varda c.1945

For a few years when Zillah had only three chavs, she and Ivor along with Vi and her young family, travelled with their parents each with their own vardas and grais. Auntie Vi was like a second mam to the chavs especially when they were little. Zillah found another photograph of another varda with her brothers Lawrence and Lias and their friend Jack Toogood who would in the future be the father of Tina Marie's best friend Martha.

Then a photograph of another varda with her younger sister Edna with her older girls brought fresh memories of her life down the lanes in those good old days when they still had the old horse drawn vardas and she went hawking with the chavvies, selling flowers, and charms and telling fortunes for money to buy food for the family. Some farmers let her have meat on a Saturday that would be cheaper than the butchers. There was a shop where she bought broken biscuits and a man at the market let her have cheap bruised fruit and vegetables. At the end of her day she returned to the trailer, cooked dinner for the family, cleaned up, washed the chavvies, kissed and tucked them up in bed and asked God to bless them all.

Their Reading varda had room for her and Ivor and four chavvies but when more came along they had to purchase two trailers and store their old varda in Wales to keep it in the family. One "Bluebird" trailer was for the chavvies and was eighteen feet in length and the other, slightly shorter at sixteen feet, was for Zillah and Ivor. It was also where they did the cooking. As the children grew they got bigger trailers. She thought of the time when Ivor had sold his horse and cart and replaced them with an old-fashioned lorry to pull one of the trailers and used it to collect scrap iron, metal and old rags in Walsall. Her dad Albert sold his horse and wagon and bought a trailer and car. But she was getting ahead of herself. This was when the chavvies were getting older.

Picture 34: Bowtop caravan with Jack Toogood, Lawrence and Dempsey in the Potteries c.1951

Zillah found a photo of herself holding her first baby Ivor and then another of her dad with two of the grandchildren and despite the remembered difficulties she felt nostalgia for the lovely life she led in the 1950s. Her passion and main reason for living were her children and their

Picture 35: Rita, Edna, Miselli and Mary c.1955

children. Nothing made her happier than to hear her children being admired. She loved it when people said, "What lovely children you've got and how lovely and clean! How nice you've got the baby. How do you keep him so nice and straight?"

They often wintered with Zillah's parents and Ivor's brother and sister-in-law, Isa and Agnes Smith, in the Potteries, under a bridge in Longton or on pieces of open ground in Hanley, Tunstall or Burslem. Ivor and Isa made baskets and sold them in the factories at Christmas time.

On these waste grounds in the 1960s the chavvies played in condemned houses and pubs with Ronnie pretending to be a barman and Grace and Alan playing the piano while the others laughed and danced. "This was until the policeman came and put them all out. Then they found another old house and moved from one to another getting scrap and copper piping and piling it in an old pram. The older brothers and sisters then took it all to the scrap man to get some pennies and shillings". One day the chavvies were

Picture 36: Albert with Lias's daughters c. late 1950s

playing in an old chemist shop and they were putting old medicines and tablets into an old pot for playing with when "the policeman came and they all ran away but the little chavvies got catched and did he give them a telling off! They never went there again."

In spring, usually March, they all headed down to the Beaconside

field on the northeastern edge of Stafford. Then in May for the summertime they went further south to Evesham for scrapping and farm work picking peas, onions, strawberries, cherries, gooseberries and plums. "Though it was hard work and we had to get up very early in the morning

Picture 37: Iza making baskets c.1955

it was a holiday for us." The children loved the freedom and fun of working and playing in the orchards and fields of Worcestershire. They met up with their friends and the teenagers went to the pictures every Sunday or walked down to "The Splash", a bend in the river, for a swim. They were "lovely days to remember" when in 1971 Grace 13 years old met her future husband Riley and Dawn and Joyce met their future husbands Harry and Joe.

Picture 38: Isa and Agnes Smith
Potteries c.1954

Picture 39: Zillah and Agnes Potteries
c.1954

Picture 40: Dawn, Alan and Joyce
c.1964

Picture 41: Tina Marie, Grace and
John c.1964

One summer in the late 1960s Alan, one of Zillah's youngest, ended up in two hospitals after an accident playing in a farmer's shed. When jumping on top of a big tin drum it fell on the top of his leg, which became trapped. Grace, Rita and Miselli rescued him but they didn't want to tell Zillah because they'd get into trouble. At night he was crying with pain with a red swollen leg so Zillah took him to the village doctor who sent them away saying it was a sprain. However, it got worse so off they took him to Worcester hospital where "they said that doctor shoulda been struck off and Alan coulda lost 'is leg!" Zillah wasn't happy with the treatment there either so she demanded an ambulance to take her, Ivor and Alan to Stafford Hospital.

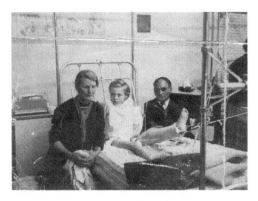

"The doctors there said it's a good job you brought him here or he'd 'av lost 'is leg!" They were very nice at Stafford giving them sandwiches and cups of tea. "The Sister said she'd pray for him as they were afraid for his leg and it might turn into TB." So Zillah prayed too and his leg got better, he was able to walk, got

Picture 42: Alan, Zillah and Ivor Stafford Hospital c.1960s

married eventually and had children and grandchildren. "He was allus a good lad, happy and contented and a very kind son."

Zillah and Ivor brought up the children to be well-mannered Gypsies. "We made sure they learned not to talk until spoken to, to say thank you and please and to get up when visitors came in their home so they could sit down. They 'ad to make sure their shoes were clean before going into anyone's home. Also they 'ad to ask the older ones if they needed any water or wood for the fire."

As young children they enjoyed plenty of freedom though. During the summer they played all day in the woods at Beaconside keeping cool by making a raft for the stream and in the winter using a pond as a skating

rink. They made their own dinner from pheasant, quail and duck eggs. To be fair to the birds they put each egg on a dock leaf and took it to the stream to see if it would float or sink. If it sank they put it back in the nest. If it floated they pierced it with a pin, made a fire and put it in the ashes to cook. Ronnie shot pigeons, partridges, and rabbits with his catapult, cleaned and

Picture 43: Olivine Clee, Ivor's sister cooking in Evesham c.1965

washed them in the stream, skewered them on a long stick and roasted them on the fire. For pudding they ate berries, crab apples and nuts including "a nut that most people don't know about from a pink thistle bush". Zillah's chavs often told her that their childhood days were full of happiness.

As they grew older they all had to do their bit going out with their mam and dad selling doormats, dropping cards for scrap and rags and selling logs. The boys went out scrapping with Ivor and the uncles, and Mary looked after the children and did the cleaning from the age of ten.

Picture 44: Ivor c.1959

Picture 45: Mary c.1960

Picture 46: Rita c.1959

Picture 47: Ronnie, Joyce, Zillah and Dawn. c.1960

Picture 48: Violet, Alan, Tina Marie and John c.1968

She and the other girls did the washing outside in a big bath of hot water on a stick fire with a washing board and mangle. Zillah remembered her children as doing their work with a happy heart enjoying the Gypsy life. "We had to live day by day and as long as they had something in their bellies we never used to bother. They never had lots of toys. Perhaps they'd have a sweet now and again. But as they grew older and things got on and they went out working, they did get a bit more. They'd help themselves, work for themselves and things became different and more modern."

Dawn, Joyce, Ronnie, Miselli and Rita all went to school together with their cousins. The three eldest, Ivor, Mary and Tony, left school when they were twelve. Grace stayed on until she was 15. They didn't need many Gorgia friends in the first school as they all stuck together with siblings and cousins. But in secondary school Grace was very shy and some children behaved "hatefully towards us". Eventually she was able to fit in when she made several friends: Constance; Ranjit; Diane; and Elizabeth. However Grace and her siblings only mixed with Gorgia friends in school and never at home.

The teachers were very good to Zillah's children, never allowed any name-calling and always included them in all school activities. Zillah remembered how Grace loved St John's Primary school in Stafford. As she was the oldest she had a lot of chores to do in the mornings before going to school. The headmaster called her into his office one day and said, "Grace you have been late nearly every morning this week. What's your reason for being late?"

Grace said, "Before I can come to school I have a lot of things to do Sir. I am the first one to get up in the mornings and my older brother, Ronnie, he makes the fire to warm the caravan. I get myself washed and dressed, then get the younger ones up and get them dressed and washed. Then I do their hair with Tina Marie's having to be plaited and Violet's curled. John and Alan's hair have to be combed and then I make their beds, which have to be folded up, and packed away. Then I make breakfast and wash everything up, wipe the kitchen down, and brush the floor. I do it so as my mother can do the other caravan and get ready to go out hawking. So I may be five minutes late Sir." When he knew the reason he gave Grace an extra ten minutes every morning and she was glad of that.

Around that time Zillah began worrying about Tina Marie's health. She had always been delicate and one day she came from school pinching her cheeks until they were red and sore. Zillah caught hold of her hands and told her not to hurt herself and spoil her lovely face. "Her dark blue eyes filled with tears an' she came out with her troubles that her face was so white she was shamed to go to school. That evening she collapsed and said she was looking down a long dark tunnel, and her eyes rolled to heaven. I rubbed her hands, face, belly and everywhere I could think to rub. Her eyes stopped rolling and she sucked in a deep breath, looked perfectly at rest and the blood came back to her face." Her doctor said she was anaemic but Zillah thought it was more than that. In fact Tina Marie had several fainting turns during her teenage years and Zillah kept a watchful eye.

The children developed their own interests and hobbies. Ronnie, Grace and Tina Marie liked to draw and saved their pennies for drawing paper and pens. Grace loved horses and when she was twelve years old living on Rickerscote farm her older brother Tony bought a big grey mare and two coloured foals for her to look after. She washed and brushed the one with fleas and calmed down the wild one. However, one day Ronnie was showing off to her how to ride the wild one and it galloped over the field and stopped sharp on the bank of the river catapulting Ronnie over her head and into the water much to the delight of Grace!

The mare was brushed until shiny and taken to market and the wild foal was sold to a man who watched Grace calm him down. The other foal was kept by Tony and given to Grace for her thirteenth birthday. "It was the one thing she always wanted and she always remembered her big brother for making her dreams come true." She trained him to do tricks and to bend down for her to mount him. He travelled with them and was tied up by the roadsides. In the summer he often swam in the river with Grace on his back.

Picture 49: Sofie, Mizelli and Rita c.1962

Zillah and Ivor were strict Gypsy parents especially when their chavvies became teenagers. They were considered to be children until they were sixteen. Then they could have different hairstyles but the girls couldn't wear make up until they were as old as twenty. Clothes had to be sensible with no short skirts or low tops. "Clothing showed how respectable you was and what respect you have for yourself." The girls weren't allowed to talk to boys they didn't know for fear of getting a bad name and bringing shame on the family. "They only went out with the boy they married and they 'ad to make sure he was the right one before they let 'im come back to their home to ask their dad's permission to court."

Despite those restrictions the teenagers had fun with their mates especially during the fruit-picking season. They loved watching the elders singing especially their mam Zillah step dancing on a wooden board and yodelling. But better still, they would get a record player and sing and jive for ages until the elders shouted at them to come in for bed. Their Uncle Dempsey bought them all of their records and played the accordion for them.

As Zillah's children grew up they kept themselves, their families and their homes clean. Zillah had always been and still was very proud of

Picture 50: Dempsey, Zillah's oldest brother, Beaconside c.1960s

them all. From the time they were little she had always kept them clean in the most difficult circumstances. They would go to houses and garages to collect water and keep it in milk churns from the farmhouses. They would wash clothes in streams and in separate bowls from the cooking, which was mostly done outside. Hot water was boiled outside for bathing in a tin bath in the varda. Separate bowls were used for hand and face washing outside. When Zillah and Ivor first started up with their young family, cooking was done on a fire outside until they had vardas with a stove inside and later trailers with gas cookers.

It wasn't an easy life. When hawking with the chavvies in a shawl there was many a time her hands felt frostbitten. "I'd have to break this privet off the hedges to put flowers on to sell. Me hands'd be that cold I couldn't break the privet. To make a livin' and look after me chavvies we'd have to walk for miles an' tramp in rain an' snow worse than we've had this winter. But it's what we were used to. We managed very well and it was a lovely way to live and I wouldn't change my life," reminisced 89 year old Zillah now snug in her trailer. Christmas was over now and Zillah had enjoyed her day over at the Hopton caravan site with Alan, John and the others and their families and with Joyce, Dawn Ronnie and Ivor and their families in their houses. But she was glad to be back in the quiet of her own trailer thinking about Christmases long ago. She noticed that nowadays she thinks more about the past than looking forward to the future and Christmas for her was always a lovely memory of a special time for the family to enjoy especially in those early days with her first born chavvies.

In her mind's eye she can see herself spending all Christmas Eve night in the varda. She'd have bathed all her chavvies and dressed them all up for bed. They used to sleep underneath her and Ivor's bed with two little doors into their bed underneath.

They'd shut the door to keep them warm but sometimes it was really hot with the heat of the fire. They had a feather mattress and a feather eiderdown, lovely and warm.

She'd say to them, "If you don't go to sleep, when you 'ang your stockin' up Santa Claus won't come an' put yer nothin' in it." So they'd hang their stockings up on the bed.

Rita'd say, "He's got a bigger one than me!" and Zillah would tell her, "They're all the same! It'll stretch bigger when yer get yer things in it. But if you don't be good, he'll bring you nothin', nothin' at all. Go to sleep now before yer Dad comes an' don't open yer eyes peepin'. If Santa sees you peepin' he won't come down the chimney!"

"How's he gonna get down our chimney?" Rita wanted to know and Zillah explained that, "He comes through the door. I'll leave it open. If you keep on talkin' none of yous'll get nothin'!"

So they'd be good and say, "Oh we won't be awake Mum, we'll go to sleep now."

"Good Night an' God bless you." And she'd tell them again, "Good Night an' don't forget, no peepin'. No openin' yer eyes an' gettin' up in the middle o' the night while me an' yer dad's asleep, wakin' us up an' lookin' for the things in yer Christmas stockin'. Yer don't do none o' that. You'll wait till it's mornin' then yer can get up an' do what yer want. Yer can sit down in the varda an' open yer stockings."

Old Zillah chuckled at the memory of hearing them whispering before four or five o'clock

"Ooh! Look what I've got! What 'ave you got Mary?"

"I've got this look Ivor. I've got sweets, oranges, apples, a doll. I've got a little book."

"I've got sweets like you Mary, a sugar mouse an' a chocolate mouse an' a little motor."

"Yes in those days they'd be really pleased, as happy as kings, with whatever they got," thought Zillah. "If they'd had a hundred pounds worth they wouldn't have been more pleased. And the lot would only cost about ten shillings."

Uncles and aunts joined them bringing gifts of toy cars, dolls, clothes or books.

Zillah and Ivor didn't exchange presents or give cards unless somebody gave them one. "I couldn't write nor read so I never used to bother. When me children was little me mam used to send a Christmas card, she could write. I used to get one o' me friends to write one for me an' I used to take it to her."

As with all aspects of the Gypsy life, there was a strict gender division of labour and Christmas Eve was no exception. After Zillah had got the chavvies to bed she did her cooking. She slowly roasted a chicken or a piece of pork, or perhaps a cockerel, or a rabbit in a big black pot sitting next to it basting it and turning it with the fat. The lid was kept on to steam and roast it at the same time. When the meat was done she took it out and did the "taters" in the same fat. Now years later she could smell it – beautiful! She'd got it roasted and then she'd only have to warm it up the next day.

On Christmas day Ivor went for a drink with the men at about one o'clock while Zillah cooked the dinner. "The chavs'd 'ave their dinner after I'd packed all their things away an' told them they could have them after dinner. An' they'd keep goin' back to get 'em out! They wouldn't leave 'em! They were that pleased with 'em they wanted 'm all the time, an' the varda bein' small you couldn't let 'em play when you were 'avin' yer dinner. Ivor'd come back about half past two. Then me an' 'im would have ours together while they played with their toys."

Zillah loved Christmas. The men went for another drink after dinner while the women had a smoke and talked around the fire outside, and looked after the chavs. They never bothered about drinking. Zillah didn't like beer, wine or any alcohol. Christmas night there were no pubs open so the women and men all sat together around the fire and they might ask Zillah to do a step dance. Boxing Day she'd be clearing up. "Sometimes I'd go out with them for a drink but it wasn't much good, I'd be worried about me children. Worried about a fire. The most important night was Christmas Eve with the chavs. We had a Christmas tree later but not when they was little. We just had a few paper chains." Zillah like most Gypsy women was very resourceful when it came to creating delicious treats in the open air, like marakli, the Gypsy cake, that smelt beautiful too. It was a big round mince pie similar to a current cake but cooked on an old-fashioned iron pan on the fire. "Roll the pastry out round, put the mincemeat in the middle put another piece on top, seal it all round like you do a pie and then put it in the pan. One side browns then you turn it over and do the other side."

Sometimes Zillah's mam put jam or marmalade in hers. Nobody told Gypsies how to cook. They had to learn it themselves by watching the old people. If it didn't turn out right the first time, they'd be bound to get it right a few times after.

Zillah's family followed the Christmas traditions in much the same way as the general population in the 1950s. When she was little her mam used to teach them Christmas carols such as "The Star of Bethlehem", "While Shepherds Watch", "Away in a Manger", and "Silent Night". They couldn't read or write so they remembered them. Zillah's own children loved carol singing on a Sunday at the chapel on the edge of a field they stayed on.

It was Jack Goodgers' Rickerscote field in Stafford. He was a very big pal of Zillah's dad when they did horse dealing. He let them stop on his farmland with their horse drawn vardas. The little chapel's still there now though it's been made into an office. Zillah remembers playing with Jack Goodgers' daughter Cynthia and riding the grais. She saw Cynthia a few years ago in Stafford and recognised her face even though she hadn't seen her since they were little chavs. She was married with children and living in Haywood.

They were so pleased to see each other, exchange their news and remember the old days. Zillah was glad the farm was still there and now owned by Cynthia's cousin Phil Goodger.

Other times they spent Christmas near Lichfield at Pipehill or Muckley Corner.

Zillah never had time for chapel on Christmas Day. "I'd be cleanin' an' cookin' all day an' the chavs'd be playin' on the grass outside. But if we were near a chapel I'd let the old 'uns take 'em but not if it was too far away. Mary used to go to Sunday Chapel an' I still got her card now! She got so many stars on it for bein' good. She had seven or eight."

Zillah's reverie was disturbed by Grace, young Abigail and John turning up with some of her favourite currant cake for tea. So she shrugged off the memories and made a cup of tea for them all. She looked around at all the Christmas cards she had in her trailer now, some of them enormous with big hearts and holly. She said to Grace and John, "Do you remember when you and Tina Marie were little we used to dress up the trailers with lots of trimmings and as you got bigger you all used to put the decorations up on the tree yourselves. I was glad when you got bigger to do it."

Grace said, "Yes Mam I remember," and John just gave her his lovely wide smile, nodded and thought his own quiet thoughts while young Abigail read all the messages in the cards.

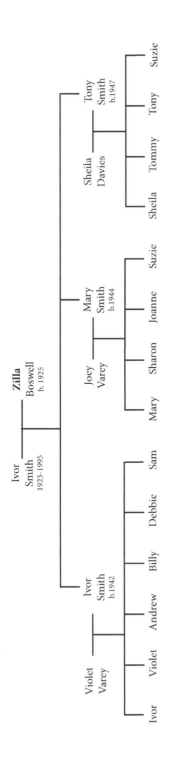

Picture 51 Smith Family Tree 1942-1980

Chapter 5

Zillah's Life on the Move 1961- 1980

"Breakin' our homes up with them big red devils"

Picture 52: Zillah Glover Street February 2015

Towards the end of February 2015 Zillah was recovering despite the cold wintery weather. She had been poorly and confined to her trailer now for several weeks and Grace and her husband Riley had stayed parked next to Zillah all this time to take care of her. They were to set off home to Temple Grafton the next day so now they had driven up to Stafford crematorium cemetery to tend the family graves. Zillah was feeling better and decided to venture into town to show her independence and to blow away the cobwebs. At nearly ninety years of age it felt good to get out by herself; she enjoyed feeling her legs work.

Sitting with her tea and oatcake in the familiar warmth of the market café, she liked watching the Gorgia folk rushing round doing their shopping. But she still couldn't fully shake off her gloomy mood and as she walked back to her trailer and waited to cross the gridlocked road coming off the big roundabout, she thought to herself, "There won't be no Gypsies much longer. They'll all be livin' in houses. It's too hard a life now. It's different now on the roads. Country lanes were different then. You could enjoy it and you could go along nice and slow with your varda and your grai."

She remembered how even into her thirties and when her first born chavvies were growing up they had still managed to maintain a traditional life on the roads. Although changes were afoot and traffic was on the increase, she and her growing family in the early 1960s still loved meandering down the lanes until they found a lane they wanted.

She loved the freedom of pulling onto a big piece of wide grass to have their dinner and from there walking around the villages nearby selling pegs and flowers, always taking the youngest baby with her.

Things were still cheap in those days too and they had good food. As long as the chavs' bellies were full, her babies were clean and sweet, and she'd done all her work she was happy.

The winter months were still difficult but she always loved the months of spring and summer. She often thought how, "spring time was allus my favourite time. First came the snowdrops and I knew it wouldn't be long before the primroses and violets'd be poking through." Summer meant hay and corn and being able to hear the wildlife, bees and birdsong. They would sometimes hunt birds but only if they were really hungry.

She loved to listen to jackdaws and what she thought of as the "laughing birds", and the noisy woodpeckers. Her favourites though were the skylarks sometimes called the "birds of dawn".

She remembered though with a shudder how all of this would soon change with the onset of new laws introduced by government to restrict the travelling way of life.

Common land was closed off from travelling families and councils were instead required to provide council run sites. However, by the mid-1960s only ten council sites had been made available for the whole of England. Furthermore, even if you had your own private land, you could only live in a caravan on it if the resident held a site license, which were rarely issued. This meant that within just a few short years the vast majority of travelling families were defined as living illegally; just four percent of Gypsies and Travellers throughout England had somewhere legal to stop.

As she opened the gate to her pitch and climbed up the trailer steps, switched on the fire and settled back in her lovely warm home she felt grateful that she now had a home to go to with no fear of being moved on. It was different when her children were growing into adults and having children of their own. She remembered all too well that the

Gorgios did some terrible things to the Gypsy and Traveller families back then. Violent evictions, some of which even led to the death of children, were resisted by Gypsy and Traveller families. She would never forget the time "when the gavvers set fire to a varda and two little raklis were burnt to death inside. They were Irish I think. They hated the Irish and never let them rest in one place for long."

By the time Grace and her older brother Alan were born in the late 1950s and the twins John and Tina Marie in 1961, their eldest siblings Ivor, Mary and Tony were young teenagers who had left school and were playing their part in the household's economy. Zillah then in her mid

30s had managed very well with organising her life around work and the children but when the twins John and Tina Marie were born she was worried that she would have twice as much work to do.

All of those old enough and still alive could remember Tina Marie and John's birth as if it had been yesterday. It was such a happy day and such a surprise. Zillah had enjoyed her pregnancy and had no idea at all she was expecting

Picture 52a: Tony c. 1960

twins. The doctors kept telling her she was going to have a small baby. The birth was a hard one compared to most of the others and it was such a relief when John was finally born into the light of the Stoke on Trent hospital delivery room. The nurses took him away from her and left her for a few minutes until she shouted for them to come back.

"Oh! I think it's twins!' she cried out to the midwife.

Her heart turned in her mouth with the shock of having two instead of one. But she was glad in her heart for the other one and five minutes later Tina Marie was born.

"Oooh! We've got another little baby and she's a girl Mrs Smith."

" Never! What another one!" Zillah cried out. Her mind was racing. What was she going to do with two babies? When she had to go out hawking and selling how was she going to manage? She couldn't carry two. She could only carry one.

As it was Alan was barely more than a baby at two years of age without having two more to carry around with her.

"Never! I can't believe it!' she was thinking. "They kept telling me I was having a small baby an' I've got two!"

"You've got a beautiful girl Mrs Smith. What do you want to call her?"

"Tina because she's so little," Zillah whispered.

John was just over five pounds and Tina just under four so she had to stay in an incubator for a little while longer. Zillah fed both of them and put Tina back in the incubator after each feed. The nurses gave her extra milk too until she was big enough. She was christened Tina Marie after the family had heard a catchy song of that name on the radio and thought it sounded nice.

Zillah —in keeping with Gypsy tradition - soon went back to work hawking around the nearby houses and beyond. Along with her toddlers Grace and Alan, she also took John wrapped snugly in a Welsh shawl, whilst her second eldest daughter Rita looked after Tina Marie. Mary and Rita had been in training for this from an early age. From the age of seven they was taught to wash up, clean, and look after the younger ones. They loved washing the babies; that was their favourite job. Their next best job was giving them a bottle. This meant that Zillah could leave Tina Marie in safe hands until her return from flower and peg selling. Zillah was very proud of all her children.

Tina Marie was a small round bundle of fair skin and fine blonde

Picture 53: Tina Marie and John
c.1963

Picture 54: Violet and Grace c.1965

curls. She looked very different from John who was darker in colouring. Rita had no trouble with her. She was as good as gold and didn't cry much as a baby unlike her noisier twin. She grew up to be a contented toddler very close to her brothers and sisters, always kind and happy to share.

In order for life to run as smoothly as possible Zillah and Ivor had their family well organised. As the children grew older, they all helped with the work. The older girls did the housework and childcare of the youngest children, Grace, Alan, the twins and baby Violet, while the older boys went out helping with the men's work.

Picture 55: Ivor and Violet c.1960

Now in her 90s Zillah, on that bright February day, was allowing herself to reminisce about how well she had brought up her children. "All my chavs have allus been brought up to look after their own. When they got old enough they cleaned the home up, kept the chavvies clean, looked after them, and gave them their dinner or whatever it was. And all my children allus cleaned their own muck up and had everything spotless."

Picture 56: Mary and Joey Varey c.1960

When a daughter married, the next one in age took over her responsibilities. When Mary got married at the age of 16, it was the turn of Rita to be the main help for her mother. Zillah had to chuckle at history repeating itself when she remembered how Mary had secretly courted Joey the brother of Ivor's wife Violet before running away to be married. "We didn't know our Mary was courtin' him! When her dad found out he said she couldn't go to the pictures with him or court him. So she cried and said,

"I can never go nowhere!"

A year later on bonfire night before the twins were born, Zillah remembered the fateful night when Mary's disappearance was discovered. It had always been Mary's job to put on the fireworks for the younger chavs but this time she'd gone out the night before and had not come back. It was a black starry night with only a sliver of a moon. "Me 'usband went lookin' for her and 'is mother went lookin' for him. We found out they'd run to Gretna Green and got married. Then they come back and told us. Me 'usband didn't like it.

I wouldn't have said nothin' against it but it was up to me 'usband."

This and Grace's were the only elopements in Zillah's immediate family. As times moved on, it became more acceptable for daughters to openly court boyfriends, who would come and ask for their hand in marriage. Most of Zillah's children went on to marry in registry offices with just a few of the later children including Tina Marie having the bigger more traditional church weddings.

Zillah dug out some more photos and came across two of her favourites. They were her beloved eldest daughter Mary with her first three daughters Mary, Sharon and Joanne.

Picture 57: Mary and baby Mary c.1964

Once again Zillah thought through the fortunes of all her children: "Ivor married Violet and had three girls and three boys. Mary married Joey Varey and she had four daughters.

Tony married Sheila and they had 4 chavs. Rita married Blossom Smith and they lived very happily

Picture 58: Mary, Sharon, Suzie and Joanne c.1970

Picture 59: Rita, Blossom and family c.1982

together with a roadful of chavs, 12 altogether. Miselli and Tony had two boys and 3 girls. Ronnie and Michelle had two of each. Dawn married Harry Lee, a Welsh Romani, and they had 3 girls and a boy. Joyce and Joe had two girls and 3 boys. Grace married Riley who was also a Smith and they had one girl and 3 boys. Alan married Julie and they had two of each. John married Sharon and they had 4 girls and a boy. Tina Marie married Tooney Neggick and had 3 chavvies. And last but not least me baby Violet married Herbert Varey, Joey's nephew, and had 4 girls and a boy. No wonder they tease me about all the people me an' Ivor helped bring into the world! Lord 'elp me I'm worn out at the thought of it!"

By the time Tina Marie had her big white wedding, there were just five of Zillah and Ivor's chavvies still living with them. Like all her daughters Tina Marie cleaned the trailers through everyday. Sometimes she got the breakfast while Zillah was getting ready to go hawking. She made their breakfast first and then get Zillah's before doing all the cleaning and washing up. Then she cleaned all the big

Picture 60: Joyce Beauty Queen at the Southend Club Stafford 1972

milk churns full of water outside the front of the trailer. "She sat in the sun talkin' and polishin' them until they shone like glass. Then she'd get herself washed after she'd had her tea.

Picture 61: Ivor and Tina Marie 1983

She was real kind an' everybody liked her. She never had a bad streak in 'er body. She was too good. She wasn't one that'd talk about anybody or call 'em names. She was allus good about everybody. She thought a lot of her brothers and sisters an' her mam and dad. Sometimes if I was goin' hawkin' she'd say,

Picture 62: Tina Marie and Martha Toogood c.1978

"I'll make the tea for when you come back Mam. I'll do some taters an' carrots an' this meat." She'd 'ave it all ready when I come back, save me doin' it."

Some days she did it all when Zillah was there. She'd say, "Sit down now an' I'll give it to you. You're not givin' it to us again, waitin' on us." She used to make tea for the whole family and wash up and clean afterwards. "And she'd wash clothes an' put 'er own things right an' look after herself too."

Tina Marie had also been a fun loving teenager into the Bay City Rollers, Davis Essex and Elvis Presley. She and her twin John were very close and had pet names for each other.

He called her "Poppet" because she was so dainty. They loved jiving together and John was so energetic a dancer jumping around that Tina Marie nicknamed him "Frog" much to everyone's amusement and the

Picture 63: Tina Marie and Tooney c.1980

Picture 64: Tina Marie, young Tina Marie and Aleisha c.1984

name stuck. So born Joseph, then as a noisy baby named John after "Big Bad John" and finally Frog!

Zillah's youngest daughters and oldest granddaughters were very close like sisters especially when they were teenagers. They loved listening to records, especially Elvis, and dancing. They dressed up in the Bay City Rollers tartan and went everywhere together walking into town from the Fairway tip in Stafford. Tina Marie was great at making a living. She would hawk flowers and would go scrapping. She was really good at cleaning the trailer and looking after the younger children. She was a proper Gypsy girl.

Tina Marie met her husband Toony Neggick at a dance. They all thought he was OK and quite nice looking and some of them are still friends with his sister Charmian who goes to the same church. However, Tooney and Zillah's family drifted apart after the death of Tina Marie even though Zillah and her siblings moved heaven and earth to keep in touch with her chavvies and look out for them.

The memory of Tina Marie – as it always did - caused Zillah's face to flush red. Tears gushed from her tired eyes falling into dark spots on the tablecloth in her Glover Street trailer. It was the death of her dad though in 1968 and then her mam in 1970 that marked the end of this era for Zillah. Her dad, Albert died aged 67 years on March 1st 1969 at Beaconside in Stafford. Zillah remembered how his death had come just

after the snowdrops had finished. "All the countryside wept for me dad, the hedges, the stones, the trees and the spring flowers. Mam picked some tiny violets for his grave. Two years later she was lying next to him. She died at the age of sixty-seven of a broken heart. If they were alive now they'd be a hundred and twelve and a hundred and ten."

Picture 65: Albert Boswell, Zillah's dad, Beaconside Field 1980s

Zillah recollected how her mam was never the same after Albert died. "She used to allus be thinkin' of him and talkin' to him like he was there. She'd say he used to get into bed with her every night. She could feel the blankets goin' up and 'im getting in bed with her. Me mam

and dad were doted to one another. One of their nice times together was when she used to read to 'im after their tea. They used to have their little off tiffs and have a little row but they soon made up. It'd be over something silly p'raps if the food wasn't done right. Anything'd start a little quarrel but they used to be alright after. She couldn't cope after he died. She'd shut her door and wouldn't let anybody in apart from me daughter Miselli."

Just then Violet (her eldest granddaughter) and Grace came home and settling down for a cup of tea they

Picture 66: Violet, Zillah's Mam c.1950s

joined in with Zillah's reminiscences taking their story into the 1970s.

This was a particularly hard time for Zillah and her family. Zillah no longer had her parents and she remembered being forced to move on by "them big red devils." These were the

Picture 67: Eviction of Gypsies at Dale Farm - www.youtube.com

cranes, tractors, diggers and excavators used by the police to forcibly evict Gypsy families from unauthorized sites.

Her daughters and oldest granddaughter, who by then were teenagers, recalled the frequent evictions, sometimes near Stafford but mostly around Wolverhampton and Walsall. One particular memory was of the riots in Bloxwich 1973. They remembered being thrown off sites and the police turning their vans over. Zillah recalled how one day "Mary and Joey were near a dog track at Walsall and all the romnis and the mushes had put a circle of tar barrels around their site and set them

Picture 68: Kenneth in his varda, Beaconside 1963

alight so the Gorgios couldn't get them. They were that desperate".

Zillah told Grace and Violet about a typical memory of that time. "We were sittin' in our trailer, an' we'd be 'avin' our food. The gavvers'd come an' tell us to move off.

They'd say, 'If you don't move off we'll fetch the tractor down an' we'll pull yer off.'

They used to back them up to the motor an' push us all up 'an pull us away. We'd be terrified to death o' them breakin' our home up with them big tractors. It was terrible.

We used to say, 'No! We 'aven't packed up'. But they wouldn't wait. They'd move us. Put us on the road an' leave us there. Sometimes they'd use to damage the trailers, the back of 'em where the pullin' bar is. They'd dent it or knock summit off it. They'd take no notice an' keep on to us all the time. They'd say, 'You've gotta move, you can't stop 'ere. You'll 'ave to find somewhere else'.

We'd say, 'Well you find us somewhere.'

'You can find your own places,' they used to say. 'You've got to get off 'ere. We've 'ad a lot o' complaints of you bin doin' this an' doin' that.' But we wasn't doin' nothin'.

Sometimes they'd summon us if we didn't get off the land an' we'd go to prison. I knew one family when they even moved a trailer when a romni was giving birth inside. They didn't care."

Zillah remembered that despite all this she and her husband Ivor were not always against the police, they knew it was the council that was ordering the evictions.

"Me 'usband would say to them, 'I know you've got yer job to do.' Sometimes they'd say, 'We don't want to do it but we've got to do it. It's the council an' there's been them complaints. Go away for a few days an' then come back an' 'ave another week.'"

Violet and Grace had heard these stories many times before and had their own memories too of these dangerous times. They both remembered the Red Devils as huge fearsome red wagons the size of fire engines with huge cranes that picked up the caravans. Their talk reminded Zillah how difficult it had been to rear her children during the evictions. When Grace and Violet were smaller and were simply asked to move on they had found it exciting and liked to go to new places. However when they were teenagers and as the evictions grew more violent they found them ever more frightening.

Their plights from this time were often reported on local TV news. Zillah remembered how Ivor's nephew Cugger (Dolphie) and his wife Wiggie and their children featured in a TV news report showing them being forced out of one of their camps in Stafford. Zillah remembered it being the Fairway Tip field off Tixall Road. Other places they were typically evicted from in Stafford were the old gas works opposite the Windmill, Rickerscote farm and Beaconside. Eventually as time wore on the families adapted and had no choice but to give in. The police would simply give them notice and Zillah's family and many others like them would pack up and leave before the Red Devils came.

Sometimes though, families simply didn't have anywhere else they could go. This was the case for Zillah's Uncle Kenneth and his twins Polly and Kensa who were given a notice to leave the Beaconsfield site in Stafford but with no place to go to. This had been their home. Kenneth - nicknamed 'Bosie" - was a well-known character among the family and the wider population of Stafford. Violet and Grace remembered with affection how when visiting Bosie they were prevented from entering his varda by his pet black crow sitting on the shafts. They'd have to wait for him to shout out to the crow, "leave 'em come in".

Grace could see these talks of the old days were hard for Zillah so she went back into her own trailer and came back with one of her books that she knew would put a smile back on Zillah's face. This book, called "The Longest Furrow: a Countryman's Reflections on Rural Life Volume 1 by Frederick Charles Waterfall (Owd Fred) a Stafford Farmer,"[9] featured a number of anecdotes about life in rural Stafford and included some stories relating to Zillah's family.

She read out one of their favourite passages about when Farmer Waterfall bought a horse named Dolly from Uncle Kenneth that would prove to be, "the only horse to ever pull a cart north bound on the M6". It was 1975 when Farmer Waterfall first heard that old Gypsy Kenneth Boswell had a horse for sale. At this time Kenneth was getting old and infirm but still lived in an old bow top wagon just outside Stafford on his own permanent site. His son and daughter, who had taken over the scrap metal business, were out collecting in their transit van when the farmer called round. The farmer recounted in his book how Kenneth was inside his wagon next to a small cast iron stove and smoking a pipe:

"Being the bloke he was, I knew he was about to "skin me" with what he wanted for the horse and gradually got round to a price three times what I had in mind."

Afterwards Kenneth agreed to throw in a four-wheeled flat wagon and a harness. A deal was struck that they were both happy with and Dolly settled into her new home with the farmer. However, no matter how hard the farmer and his daughter tried to persuade her otherwise, whenever Dolly proceeded down a road or the country lanes she persisted in her habit of walking four feet away from the kerb or hedge as she had done during her working life pulling Kenneth's wagon.

Picture 69: Kenneth, Polly and their varda, Doxey, Stafford 1963

The anecdote most loved by Zillah though was the tale about the day when Dolly and Kenneth walked along the M6. They had travelled ten miles on the regular roads as far as Penkridge searching for scrap iron when Kenneth spotted what he thought was a handy shortcut home. Being illiterate Kenneth couldn't read the signs that explained that this was the slip road onto Junction 13 of the M6. Once on it they had intended to travel the five miles to junction 14 where his camp was close by. They managed to trot along merrily until about half way along when they were stopped by the police and escorted the rest of the way. Farmer Waterfall in his book noted with relish, "This incident was reported on all the television news stations that night and in all the newspapers the

74

following day as well. Dolly was the first and only horse to use the M6 motorway."

Slipped inside Farmer Waterfall's book was also a newspaper cutting from The Staffordshire Newsletter dated April 18th 2013. Grace read out the section called "Times Gone By" that had a photo of Zillah's uncle Kenneth standing by his caravan in 1963. The headline was "Gipsy (sic) Ken's joy of the open road"

The text read,

"Doxey born gipsy(sic) Kenneth Boswell, 78, was facing another move in 1963 when Stafford magistrates gave him order to move his gipsy caravan from land at Beaconside a few hundred yards from the RAF Stafford Camp. Mr Boswell who described himself as a tatter, collecting and selling old rags and scrap declared there is nowhere for me to go. I would die if I had to live in one place. I love this open air."

Even Bosie was not safe from evictions. After their reminiscences Violet left for home, Grace retired to her trailer and Zillah prepared to go to bed. She chuckled fondly at the memory of Uncle Kenneth and how she used to play with his twins one of whom, Polly, single and childless, still lived in a trailer in a very small site near Beaconside.

She is either two months older or two months younger than Zillah (they disagree over it).

Zillah hasn't seen her for years as Polly keeps herself to herself apart from going to Zillah's son Ronnie at weekends. Yet she and Polly had been quite close during the war riding their bikes together. Zillah remembered how Polly even at the age of 70 years old had still loved riding her bike to visit her, Dempsey and Lias at Glover Street, but not any more.

As she drifted off to sleep Zillah's thoughts returned to those free days of the 1950s before the evictions that came to mark her adult life. She couldn't help but lament that her early fears had come true; the traditional travelling Gypsy way of life had come to an end.

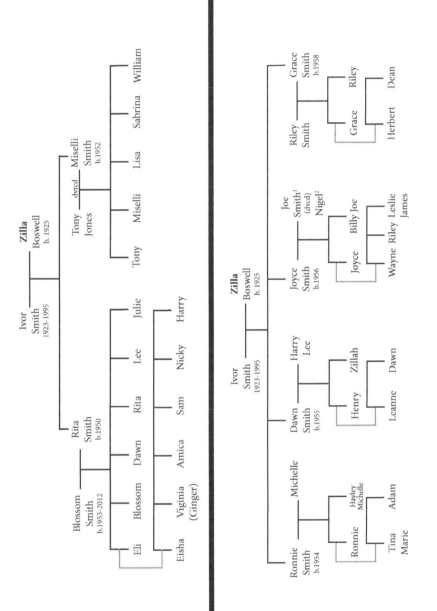

Picture 70 Smith Family Tree 1980-2000

Chapter 6

Zillah: The Gypsy Queen 1980-2015

"I can look anybody straight in the eye an' smile an' say I look on the bright side and not on the dull side."

Picture 71: Zillah aged 90 in 2015

Zillah was now in her 91st year. It was early November 2015 just over a year since Zillah's brother Dempsey had died at the age of 87 years. She still missed him every day. He had been the last of her brothers with Lias and Lawrence having died a few years before and her older sister Violet after them. She had experienced the loss of so many loved ones throughout her life that the loss of her last brother seemed particularly hard to bear. She had gone to the funeral of her daughter Tina Marie in 1988 and that of her husband Ivor in 1995, but she couldn't bring herself to go to Dempsey's funeral, "coz I couldn't see him and he couldn't see me. He was my last brother."

As she was sorting out her photos she came across a lovely picture of Dempsey playing the accordion and her father Albert with his car and trailer that had replaced his horse and varda.

They transported Zillah back to the years spanning the 1980s and 1990s and despite the good times she remembered they also brought with them some of the most difficult times for her to endure. Her parents had both died in the 1960s and in the 1990s Zillah lost her husband and her young daughter Tina Marie.

Life as a travelling Gypsy was proving ever harder during this time with increasing restrictions on travelling and stopping. In 1996 a reporter Amber Henshaw interviewed her for a report in the Stafford Chronicle August 9th 1996. The headline was "Travelling tradition nearing a standstill says Zillah". (Appendix 5)

By the time her eldest daughter, Mary, was 40 years old in 1984 their lives were markedly different from that of her namesake, her great grandmother Mary. Even though Mary's chavvies still knew the Gypsy life, Zillah back then still worried about how future generations would survive. "Gypsy life was good in me young days but it was dying in the 1980s barring the old people like me who still kept the Gypsy routine. As for the young generation it seemed to be dying off with them. They didn't know a lot o' the Romany life - not a good many o' the young uns that was growing up then."

Picture 72: Ivor, Chantelle, Zillah and Julie c.1980

Zillah blamed these changes on the way in which travelling families were forced to live on council sites. "It's the ruination of the life of the Gypsies you know. You can't go on the commons and you can't pull in no lanes no more. You're on these camps and if you leave you can't get back on so you go to another one and sometimes they're full up." Zillah had been particularly worried about Tina Marie's children, who, after her death in 1988, were being brought up by their father Tooney and a Gorgia woman in a house.

Tina Marie's short life and death in 1988 illustrated the Gypsy spirit living on despite the difficulties and changes in modern life between the 1960s and 1990s. Zillah grieved not only for the death of Tina Marie but also for the creeping death of the old Gypsy lifestyle brought about by changes in the Gorgia society around them. During this time increasing

Picture 73: Sharon's mam Diddy, John, Sharon Marie and Zillah c.1983

industrialisation and the growth of urbanisation, the motorcar and the media were undermining the traditional ways for Gypsies to make a living and to contribute to the culture and economy of the nation. The racism against Gypsies in schools, the loss of traditional stopping places, the violent evictions and travellers' pitched battles with police all wrought terrible consequences on the Gypsy way of life and individual Gypsies like Grace, Mary, Tony, Alan, John who were beginning to raise their young families.

Tina Marie was a Romany who did not survive beyond the age of 27 yet she educated her three children in the traditional ways to enable them to continue living the Gypsy life. The same can be said for Mary and all of Zillah's children but the younger generation found it

Picture 74: Tony and Sheila's wedding day May 25th 1968

increasingly difficult to live the Gypsy life as they become influenced by the Gorgia lifestyle so strongly pushed on them in schools and through the media.

In 1989, a year after they had lost Tina Marie, Zillah and Ivor moved on to Tony's Hopton site on the edge of Stafford and in the early 1990s, Zillah and her husband Ivor were settled at the Fishponds Gypsy Caravan site in Featherstone along with the family of Mary and their son-in-law Joey Varey. Zillah would often shop at Penkridge market nearby and remembered how the country roads she walked along were lined with hedgerows filled with cheerful berries, crimson and purple, jostling with russet leaves.

Situated opposite Featherstone prison on the way to Wolverhampton, the site was surrounded by a tall hedgerow and was accessed through a small gap in the hedge.

Picture 75: Zillah and Ivor at Fishponds Caravan Park 1995

Once inside there was a distinct change of atmosphere from the world outside. During the day while the men were out at work, with their vans and trucks, the spacious grey square could feel a bit bare despite the trailers.

In those days though Zillah found it as good a site as any. The grass verge reminded her of being by a lane like in the old days. Whilst living there, she and Ivor

Picture 76: Dawn and Mary at Fishponds Caravan Park 1995

bought a new trailer. It was in a quiet spot at the far corner of a large open gravelled space around which were pitched about fifteen to twenty more bright and shiny trailers. The site had a peaceful relaxed atmosphere with rarely a sound to be heard.

Once on site, nothing could be seen beyond the hedgerow that surrounded them. There was a glimpse of a field behind

Zillah's trailer but that was all that could be seen of the outside world. There was a fence behind them on the far side but behind that were more caravans, static ones occupied by Gorgios who used to be house dwellers. That was the only sign of human life in this quiet little corner of Staffordshire.

Picture 77: Ivor, John, Saley Smith, Zillah's nephew, Jimmy Varey (Mary's brother in law) and Ivor at Fishponds Caravan Park c.1994

Zillah did not know everyone on the site. She would often think "People 'ere keep themselves to themselves." Although Joey, her son-in-law, and the others had decided to buy the land they were not successful in securing the necessary caravan site license. They made it into a good site and kept it clean and respectable, but she remembered how "the council kept turning it down and wouldn't classify it because of complaints from the residents but there was hardly anybody livin' round 'ere, apart from these next door on the other site an' the prison." Zillah remembered how sometimes the prisoners could be heard "shoutin' real angry like with terrible swear words. We didn't like the chavs to hear it. But we did get the dustbin man comin' there in the end. We never used to. We'd 'ave to take the rubbish ourselves."

Mary, Joey and their family and some of their siblings families were living on the site and were made up of four generations. One of Ivor and Zillah's great nieces, Emma, could still speak a few Romany words and was proud of her Gypsy heritage. She had tried living in a house but had hated it and ended up sleeping in a trailer parked in the garden. Zillah remembered how

Picture 78: Young Dawn, Lianne and Emma at Fishponds Caravan Park 1997

Picture 79: Young Zillah and Suzie at Fishponds Caravan Park 1997

one of her granddaughters, Miselli's daughter Sabrina, used to like coming out with Romani jib words when Gorgias were around just to torment them. She liked having "no cares, no worries an' being free. More free than those Gorgio kids at school in their little houses an' flats cooped up watchin' tele all the time." Sabrina often said to Zillah, "As long as there's food in the cupboard we're OK. We see different people all the time an' you never get sad if you leave a place 'cause you know you can go back. Some people find it a hard life but we're brought up for it so I suppose we don't know any different."

Zillah thought about Sabrina now in 2015 grown up with children of her own living in her own house in Newark surrounded by other Gypsies. Unlike some of her siblings who live 45 miles away on a site in Peterborough, she likes living in a house "especially in the winter with a warm toilet seat!" She has a trailer on her drive and although there's nowhere to pull in nowadays she likes to live as a Gypsy despite living in a house.

Zillah and Ivor had moved on to the Fishponds site in 1991 to be with their family after they had lost their daughter Tina Marie. Her memories of that time are tinged with sadness; it was a time of mourning. Tina Marie died aged 27 years on 26th February 1988 when her baby Tooney was eleven months old and her daughters were toddlers. She was buried on 3rd March 1988 in Stafford at a big Gypsy funeral with Gypsies travelling from as far away as Wales, London and Newcastle on

Tyne. There were so many people that the police stopped the traffic in Stafford to let all the cars, vans, trailers and wagons through to the crematorium.

Zillah remembered how "it began a lovely sunny day but when we was follerin' the hearse and just comin' from the funeral it came over as misty and foggy as the dreams of the mulla. The gavvers had to guide the motors an' we thought we couldn't get no further. We'd never seen nothin' like it before. But when we reached the cemetery at Beaconside the sun come out on where she was to be buried. It shined and it bloomed right on her grave. It shined lovely it did. It was so beautiful. I never seen such a lovely day in me life. It were handsome. It were like the Lord was with her. The sun was shun right on her as she was goin' down an' it was real hot for ages an' ages an' was full on her. And on me dad it did the same. Remarkable innit? I'd seen her laid out and she was handsome, done up ever so nice. She was really back to herself. Nice an' young like she was before she got married. Really beautiful she was." Whenever Zillah saw snowdrops they reminded her of Tina Marie and her snow-white face.

A few short years later, Zillah went on to lose her husband Ivor in 1995. In Zillah's world if a man's wife dies and he's got children he'll marry again. However if a romni loses her rom they rarely marry again, although she knew a few who had over the years. Zillah never wanted to marry again herself after Ivor died. She never wanted any other rom. She kept to the one man and was always really proud of him. They were devoted to each other just like her mam and dad had been, "I know how me mam felt when she lost me dad because I feel the same now I've lost my Ivor."

Joey and Mary managed to keep the site going for another five years after the death of Tina Marie. Zillah and Ivor continued to live there initially and then after Ivor's death just Zillah. Joey wouldn't let Zillah pay rent. "He was very good to me", thought Zillah. "One year Joey had to pay a £2000 fine

Picture 80: Glover Street 1990s © Dawn Jutton
http://www.dawnjutton.com

Picture 81: Zillah's next door cabin, Glover Street 1990s © Dawn Jutton http://www.dawnjutton.com

for us living on 'is own land! Then he won in the court and we thought we were alright but no, the council took it to the head man of the government, the Secretary of State, an' he turned it round and said we've got to go. They sent us a letter tellin' us we've got to be off by the 28th of that month. And we didn't know where we were gonna go. We couldn't go on the roadsides like we used to do. But had to find somewhere. And if we didn't go they'd put an injunction an' it'd spoil it for us ever comin' back. They told us if we went then we might be able to come back in a couple o' year's time."

At this time Mary and Joey and other Gypsies who were under threat of eviction from their own land were finding it increasingly difficult to survive as Travellers in the United Kingdom. Like many other Travellers over the past few years they considered moving to Europe and especially Germany after the fall of the Berlin Wall in 1989. Joey and Mary felt their skills and contribution to society would be recognised and welcomed in the new Germany.

They had already made several visits and believed an easier living could be made over the Channel. This never came about. "Mary and Joey's lot went back on the road lookin' for a council site and back I came to Glover Street."

At that point in her remembrance her daughter Dawn came into the trailer back from the shops and began cooking some stew and dumplings for Zillah's tea. She saw her mam was looking sad and asked her what was up. Zillah told her she was thinking about

Picture 82: Ivor and grandson Henry picking beans in Evesham 1990

Ivor, Mary and Tina Marie . "You can see the sadness o' me life in these tears down me eye. Sometimes I get just 3 tears out of one eye an' I leave 'em there when it 'appens as I know it's Tina Marie comfortin' me an' tellin' me not to cry an' life's got to go on. Today is the first time for ages I've wept more than 3 tears since my lovely daughter died but a lake o' tears would never be enough."

Zillah didn't like her children seeing her crying for fear of upsetting them so she pulled herself together and got ready to eat her tea. Dawn decided for her mam's sake to move on the conversation and she had her own thoughts about those times in the 1980s and 1990s. In the early 1990s Dawn's dad, her son Henry and other family members were still able to take trips to Evesham to pick fruit and vegetables. However, things got worse for them all by the very end of the century. Everyday life was more difficult than in previous decades with places to stay getting increasingly hard to find. The Gypsies had to buy land on which to live, as there were no sites and they could no longer travel the lanes and byways.

Zillah told Dawn she remembered "a mush (man) in Lichfield who had a piece o' land in Fradley near Lichfield. It was near a railway line, out of the way, hidden with about nine or ten vardas on it. He 'ad made it into a beautiful site with water laid on, very clean and tidy with room for two or three families. But the council said 'e had to close it and they'd all be evicted. If only the councils could build a site in the town and then say, 'if you want to leave this site, there's another site in another town, you can go to that then we could still do our travellin'. That's how they oughta make 'em. Not sites where you live there an' not move off 'em.

They oughta be travellin' sites so you can travel from one site to another."

Dawn had to agree. When they got evicted they sometimes only had the lay-bys to pull in to.

Zillah said, "How could

Picture 83: Ivor making wooden flowers

me an' Ivor have managed like that at our age, being moved on all the time? Ivor had a stroke and needed lookin' after.

He worried terrible about where we were gonna go an' never stopped askin'. He rambled on' and it made him ill. He fell down and hurt all his leg. He should have been looked after not moved about. In the old days we looked after our old folks down the country lanes and never bothered the authorities with our problems. I paid poll tax but got nothin' for it only what Mary an' Joey had done on our site. I pay council tax now but I don't even get the heating allowance because I don't live in a house."

Picture 84: Zillah aged 70 1995

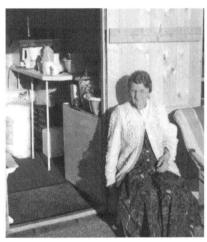

Picture 85: Zillah aged 71 Glover Street 1996

Picture 86: Zillah aged 78 Glover Street 2003

Picture 87: Zillah aged 82 Glover Street 2007

Zillah remembered how she and Ivor always earned their own money, "an' never got anythin' off the government at all. But I was told I could get a pension for me 'usband. The lady told me I should get more because he had to be looked after. He didn't know what he was doin' an' he forgot things. I'd bin thinkin' I want to try for

Picture 88: Zillah aged 84 with her friend Annie Cartwright, Glover Street 2009

them to find me a house but what d'ya think Ivor said? I said to him, "I'm gonna get meself a nice little old pensioner's bungalow. He said, "I don't want to go in no houses. You can go if you want. I'm not goin' in. You can leave me 'ere!"

By the time Ivor died in 1995 they had a pension for them both but it wasn't much.

Zillah still had her pension today but it didn't go far. "A bottle o' gas costs me twenty odd pound an' I 'ad to keep it on night an' day over this last winter. It only lasts just over a week. It's a struggle. You can't buy the best o' foods."

Once Zillah had eaten her dumpling stew Dawn left. Zillah changed into her pyjamas, settled back down with her TV programmes and felt grateful to have so many of her family living in or near Stafford. She had moved back to Glover Street in 1996 after losing Ivor and after the whole family had to vacate their land at

Picture 89 Zillah aged 89 Glover Street May 2014

Fishponds Caravan Park. The family set her up in a nice trailer with a wooden hut at the side of it. Although she's had a few more trailers since then she hasn't moved from this plot.

Dawn, her fourth daughter and seventh child is the one who has lived nearest for the last twelve years in an old terraced house in Stafford with her husband Harry.

Picture 90: Zillah and John, Glover Street May 2001

Zillah knew she was very happy there and would never live in a trailer again "with all the mither of going outside for this and that".

Zillah's eldest child, Ivor, was also living nearby in a council house in Doxey. He and his wife Violet(nee Varey) were forced to move there in 2000 due to the absence of any sites and his poor health. Although he was settled there and his younger sister Joyce and brother Ronnie also lived in council houses nearby, he often regretted having moved into a house.

A religious man, Ivor used to drive every week to the Christian Life and Light Travellers' church in Willenhall but now goes to their church in Rugeley. Before that he went to the Travellers' church at the village hall in Hopton and later a bigger hall in Great Haywood. He and other members of the family have been many times to "Life and Light" Conventions held in large tents alongside other Gypsies.

Three of Zillah's other children, Tony, John and Alan lived with their families nearby on a Gypsy caravan site in Hopton, a village between Stafford and Weston, but others were scattered further afield in Warwickshire, Leicestershire and Lincolnshire. They were self-employed laying driveways with tarmac or paving slabs, gardening, tree-work and sometimes

Picture 91: Zillah and Tony c. 1988

recycling of scrap metal. There was plenty of work locally and John in particular had more than enough in the summer months. John and all of her children took turns helping Zillah take care of the housework inside and out of her trailer.

The summer of 2015 had been a busy time for Zillah's family and feeling cold on this November night, she was looking forward to enjoying the warm weather again in the Spring. She was determined to make it to her 91st birthday in March of the next year. Although it always took a while to warm up, compared to trailers she's had in the past this one was as good as it could get for her in her old age. John and her other sons had bought it a few years ago. It had been left over from the emergency accommodation provided to the Gorgias flooded out of their homes in Worcestershire.

Like a typical mobile home, it had a sink and taps and a small toilet cabinet.

When Zillah awoke the following morning Grace and her husband Riley had pulled up just outside Zillah's gate and wired up to the electricity outlet. They were to stay for as long as the council allowed for them to look after Zillah once again until she was back on the mend. Dawn had taken Zillah for a scan of her heart the previous week, which showed it had "grown big" but otherwise nothing was untoward.

Zillah was still in her dressing gown and very out of sorts with Grace for making her get up. These days she liked to stay warm in bed until midday and was now having some difficulty breathing. As Grace was preparing lunch she had plenty on her mind and was especially concerned about her daughter and son who both had celiac disease.

They were no longer being monitored properly because of the NHS cuts and though one of the GPs had told her son to start eating a normal diet again this had made him ill.

To cheer herself and her mam up Grace had brought some more pieces of writing from Zillah's great great granddaughter Abigail to read out loud. They expressed a love of her life as a Gypsy girl living in Temple Grafton. One called "My Life as a Gypsy by Abigail Birch Age 10 " described how she enjoyed living close to nature, enjoyed her friendships at school, went to all the clubs and was learning the violin. Abigail was full of enthusiasm for her Gypsy life and also for being part of life in an English Gorgia village. (Appendix 4)

Grace's grandsons who were a bit older than Abigail also enjoyed the Gypsy life and had done well at the village primary school but they were considerably less enthusiastic about secondary school. After starting secondary school, neither lasted any longer than two weeks. After all the preparations and getting of uniforms the boys set off each morning for school with heavy hearts and a deep sense of foreboding. They told their mothers they didn't want to go any more as they couldn't use the toilets in school. The older children were in the toilets "dealing or taking drugs and looking at images on their phones." The older of the two had his jumper stolen. When the mothers complained to the teachers at the school they were told to expect this at a secondary school and that it was the pupils' responsibility to look after their own belongings. When the mothers said they would take the boys out of the school the teachers did not try to stop them. They were now getting monthly home tuition provided by the local Traveller Education Service. Thankfully Abigail had started a different secondary school in Stratford that September and loved it.

Grace, like Abigail, but unlike her mam, had also enjoyed school at the Riverside Secondary Modern school for girls in Stafford. She often wondered whether the reason why her parents allowed her to stay on until she was 16 years at secondary school was because there were no boys there. She had been keen for her own children to go to school and especially her nieces and nephew, the young Tina Marie, Aleisha and Tooney the chavvies of Tina Marie. Zillah, Grace, and her sisters had always done their best for them after the death of their mother. Now young Tina Marie and young Tooney had grown up and were settled. Tina Marie was now a hairdresser and married to Garnet a Gorgia man.

They have a baby called Jacob and live happily in a house in Willenhall. Her brother Tooney worked as roofer up and down the country and was still living with his dad in another house in Willenhall.

Tina Marie's middle child, Aleisha, however had died some eleven years before on January 11th 2004. It had been just before the birth of Grace's granddaughter Abigail, and both Grace and Zillah remembered it well. She was aged just 16 years. She had been found in a ditch in a road called Heath End in Warwick two days after her death.

Picture 92: Mary and Zillah, Fishponds Caravan Site 1997

Grace had always had a sense of foreboding about that place every time she drove past Heath End from either side of the road. "I just had to look down that road I don't know why - it's like I was drawn to it. Years after I had a terrible shock when the police came and told me that my niece was found there. I still feel me sister Tina Marie sending me messages about her chavvies. Sometimes I've woken up with these strong feelings and sat on the trailer and looked up at the stars and wondered what was wrong with the chavvies. I would go to see them the next day and they always had a problem. Once Tina Marie appeared to my daughter in a mirror in a motorway service station and she felt like she was being warned. She had an accident straight after but survived. It was like she'd been warned and was being watched over."

The death of Aleisha affected them all in the family. When Mary the eldest aunt of Aleisha died a few years later in 2007 times were very sad. Mary had been the eldest daughter of Zillah and had been a second mother to all the siblings. They gave her the nickname "Queenie". A big part of their lives was lost when Mary died. If any of them had any problems they could always talk to Mary and she told them the truth.

She gave them Christmas presents in their stockings. She always had a smile when she saw them. Zillah expressed their sorrow and the grief of Joey, Mary's widower, in a poem called "We'll Meet Again"

"We're all hurt and can't believe she's dead.
She was such a beautiful person.
Joey says he won't live long.
"When I'm down there in the earth
With my lovely wife I'll be alright"

(See the whole poem in Appendix 4)

Picture 93: Zillah, Glover Street 2015

Grace still talked to her big sister Mary when she was troubled about something. Her current concern was the continuing problem with her family's caravan site in Temple Grafton. The temporary planning permission granted in 2012 for them to use their small piece of land as a site for their five trailers had come up for renewal the previous March. When they first bought the land from a builder it was overgrown and covered in rubble. They cleared it and had portaloos delivered ready for habitation. The next morning, however, an enforcement officer put a stop notice on the delivery. Mary and her family had to go to court and pay the expensive fees required for a barrister. Mary recalled how, "the judge couldn't get over it! He said, 'You've brought these people to court over a toilet! What do you want these people to do? They need a toilet-it's obvious they need a toilet in a field!'"

Following the application, they found out just before Zillah's 90th birthday that they were granted consent but still only temporarily. They were granted just three years. While relieved for the initial reprieve they still felt angry that the consent was not permanent; in a two years time they would have to go through the whole process again and spend yet more money.

Zillah felt for her daughter. All their problems were nothing new to her. She had been through some tough times in her life, but she smiled when she thought about how her ever-growing extended family called her the "Gypsy Queen". She knew they were partly teasing her but that they also meant it as a sign of respect. For her it was natural to do what she could to take care of her remaining children, grandchildren and great grandchildren. Now she was aware that they were taking care of her.

She was proud that her sons and daughters and grandchildren were not giving up on living the Gypsy life. Despite all the obstacles that she and her family still faced and the losses they had had to endure over the years, she still had hope. She often told herself, "At the end of it all I can look anybody straight in the eye an' smile an' say I look on the bright side and not on the dull side. I'm proud o' me chavs an' I'm proud of all me family and me Gypsy life. "

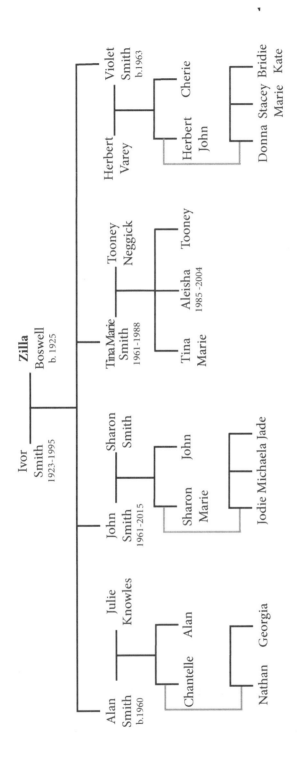

Picture 95: Smith Family Tree 2000-2016

Epilogue

"You are the strongest woman I have ever known and I'm proud to have you as my mother-in-law".

A few weeks later the death of John, her son, in late November 2015 was broken to Zillah by her stricken children and she took to her bed. On the morning of his funeral on 3rd December 2015 her trailer door was locked against her family and the dark. She covered her head with the sheet and imagined one dark day in the little black month of February nearly 100 years ago. She felt for her long dead Granny Mary. She now knew what it was like to lose a son.

Throughout the journey of writing this book, I had become a close family friend and when I called to see Zillah on that sad day, she asked that I attend the funeral instead of her. So I did.

Several hundred people were gathered at Stafford Crematorium around the front of the chapel, as it wasn't possible for everyone to be inside. They were listening on the loud speaker to Pastor Swale of the Gypsy Traveller Church based in Willenhall and Rugeley. He was John's son-in-law. John's open van had been made into his hearse and was parked outside decorated with flowers on each side red and white spelling out husband, father and brother.

The order of service had a photo of John on a boat on the Sea of Galilee arms raised to the sky asking for God to bless his granddaughter. That very next day she learnt to ride a bike. Inside was a picture of John and Sharon with all their grandchildren and another with him (aka Frog) dancing at a church social.

The coffin had been taken from the van into the chapel to the song of Big Bad John and now Pastor Swale was telling us why Joseph got his nickname John. As a baby he cried more than his twin Tina Marie so they sang a song that was in the charts at the time. He also explained why the close family had a touch of red on their clothing. This was the story about one Friday night when his next eldest brother Alan borrowed one of John's favourite shirts without asking. It was his best red one that he wore to dances. Alan drank too much cider, which was out of character, and ended up being sick all over John's shirt. He was so scared John would kill him so he rolled it up in a ball and hid it. John the next day couldn't find his shirt for the dance that night and asked Alan if he'd had it. Alan made a half vow saying he hadn't but had his fingers crossed behind him. John wasn't convinced and he searched for and found the shirt, washed, dried and ironed it and wore it to the dance.

People were listening and there were low murmurs and conversations going on and the occasional "shush". There were a few chuckles at the story that was obviously well known in the family. The closest families were inside and many of the people outside were extended family, friends and colleagues. Everybody was in black with many men dressed in dark suits and a good number of women in full-length fake fur coats – many with pushchairs and babies. After the story of John's shirt "Unchained Melody" was played. It was very sad with many quiet tears from the people around me. Another Gorgia friend of John, David Parker who runs a roofing business, stood with me and we exchanged a few whispered stories about John. David had known John for 35 years. He had seen him twice over the previous few weeks as David did land deals for him. John drove a hard bargain by the sounds of it much to David's amusement and admiration. This latest deal was to sort out a piece of land for storage and his vans.

The Pastor described John as "a man's man, a joker and a bit of a torment who played a great many tricks on his brothers and male relatives." He was also very kind and would give a helping hand to anybody in need. John loved and was very proud of all his family and was loved by them. John was a strong, strapping man who kept fit, worked hard and went to the gym regularly. Like many a kushti mush he took pride in his clothes and appearance.

John's grown up son, "Little John", read out a poem of three rhyming verses - reflecting on the strong loving bond between father and son even though they did not always see eye to eye. (Appendix 3)

The pastor talked about the love John had for his wife Sharon and what a good wife and homemaker she was. Their last evening together when he was having pains in his chest like heartburn she made him some hot chocolate. They talked and had a nice evening together and he told her that he loved her. John had been converted to Christianity and was "born again" four years before when he had joined the Light and Life Gypsy Church. Last year he went with the church to Jerusalem.

The Pastor consoled the congregation that it was a good way to die with no suffering with the words "I love you" so recently expressed to Sharon. John believed he was going to a better place than here on earth and we were to think of this as not goodbye but "see you later". His twin Tina-Marie, sister Mary, niece Aleisha and Uncle Dempsey were there in heaven waiting for him. We would be with them ourselves one day. For those of the congregation who were not of this way of thinking he hoped we'd take away a bit of John's belief into our hearts.

The crowd parted for the big white coffin to be carried out by six male pallbearers and followed by the close family in a long procession to a copse of tall trees. A huge crowd gathered as the coffin was lowered into the grave. A young woman Jade - his pregnant youngest daughter - was sobbing held up by the women around her. Sharon dropped the first flower and soil into the ground. The pallbearers, Alan and other big strapping men, hugged each other very upset and shook each other's hands. There was a carpet of flowers already by the grave and people brought more wreaths to join them. The grave of John's twin Tina Marie was nearby also covered in flowers.

On our return to Zillah's trailer she told us she'd had "a happier morning than you lot", thinking about John, seeing him in her mind's eye and talking to him. She was exhausted and disgruntled because people kept arriving at different times of the night and she hadn't got much sleep. She wasn't pleased when Grace, Rita, Alan, his wife Julie and Zillah's grandson Eli went back to the cemetery to sort out and arrange the flowers at the grave. However, she took some comfort from Julie's departing words to her that "you are the strongest woman I have ever known and I'm proud to have you as my mother-in-law".

While they were away Zillah spent a long time talking to me about John who she believed was in heaven. The last time she'd seen him was three Saturdays before after the funeral of her granddaughter Suzie's husband.

"He wasn't his usual self sitting here in the trailer quiet and almost in a trance. He told me he loved me so much it was almost too much and that was the last time I saw him. Three Saturdays ago was the last time I spoke to him. He was on the phone with Sharon in the car. They was on their way home from their daughter's. We talked for the last time and said we loved each other. I told 'im to take it easy and not go to work on the Monday. But he did go and came home and got the heartburn and pains in his chest. Next morning he had a heart attack and they got an ambulance to Stoke hospital. They told us it was too late and he was brain dead but Little John didn't believe he was dead so they put him on a machine until they told us he was dead last Thursday. Alan and Julie took me to see him before that. It was horrible to see him with all the wires. It didn't look like my John. At the chapel of rest it didn't look like him at all. Not like that photo you've brought me - that's how John really looked." On her table John was almost present beaming out his lovely smile as he was sitting next to Zillah in her trailer a few months after her 90th birthday.

Picture 94: Zillah aged 90 and John 2015

Grace and Rita returned from the cemetery with the news that John had had the last laugh. A flower from one of the wreaths had jumped out in front of Grace. She took this as a sign from John. Also one of the floral crosses had dropped down and when they put it back it fell apart. Another sign. Grace had already told me yesterday about how all the numbers added up. John and his twin Tina Marie were born on the 27th July. She died on 27th February and he fell ill on the 27th November. They took comfort from any sign of light and hope.

Their way of dealing with the death of someone who was so much loved shows us the power of this family's resilience and their determination not to be beaten. Many of their Romany Gypsy traditions still live on and yet they live their lives entwined among the house dwelling population. This is not story of a life carved out separately from the rest of the world. Their loves and losses are ours too.

Appendix 1

The Millennials March 20th 2016

91 years ago on this day Zillah was born. Thanks to her and Ivor 13 children, 61 grandchildren, 194 great grandchildren and 40 great great grandchildren (at the last count) came into existence. Their family is one of the biggest Gypsy families in England. Zillah continues to be the Matriarch of this family who still live and work in

Picture 96: Zillah and Alan on March 20th 2016

the Midlands, Peterborough, Wigan, Much Wenlock, Wolverhampton, Brierly Hill, Willenhall, Oxford, Gloucester, Evesham, Pershore, Stratford upon Avon, King's Winford, Doncaster, Market Harborough, Burton upon Trent, Cannock and, of course, Stafford.

On this day Zillah is in good spirits and feeling well as some of her family, mostly from Stafford, came over to her trailer to spend the previous evening watching old family videos. They had such a laugh! They watched Zillah at her 80th birthday fancy dress party in 2005 singing, step dancing and even break dancing with Alan one of the grandchildren! Now

Picture 97: Joyce, Zillah, Miselli, Dawn and Rita, Glover Street March 20th 2016

all her daughters and daughter-in-law Julie arrived to take her out for lunch at a restaurant in town. Zillah looked very elegant as did they all in their black attire worn in mourning for John.

Rita and Miselli travelled from Peterborough where their extended families all live in a mix of council and privately owned houses, and Gypsy caravan sites. Rita has seven daughters, five sons, 45 grandchildren and 13 great grandchildren. She lost her husband Blossom three years ago and lives with her sons Sam and Harry in a bungalow near some of her children. It faces the big council site on the edge of Peterborough that is owned by the father in law of Blossom. Rita's son Blossom and daughter Eisha live on the site. Another son Nicky rents a house in Peterborough. Her eldest Eli lives on his own site in Spoden and Dawn lives on a council site. Lee, Julie, Ginger and Aneka all live in houses with their families.

Picture 98: Rita and Blossom c.2011

Miselli and her son William live on the Peterborough site with her daughter Lisa. Her other son Tony and family live in houses nearby. Her daughter Sabrina lives in a house in Newark and Miselli her eldest lives on a site in Wigan. Altogether Miselli has five children 23 grandchildren and one great grandchild. Sabrina's two youngest children Anastasia and Isaac attend the local primary school and her eldest daughter Sabrina has been home educated since leaving primary school.

Sabrina's four children went to primary school but they didn't stay long at secondary school and now have home tutors provided by the local Traveller Education Service who visit intermittently and leave them 'piles of books' covering English, mathematics, science and other subjects. Two of the girls say

Picture 99: Miselli's daughter, Sabrina, Peterborough March 2001

they can read but don't understand the maths.

Zillah's youngest daughter Violet travelled from Burton-on-Trent where she lives with her husband Herbert who is Violet's brother-in-law Joey Varey's nephew. They live with Cherie and Herbert John, two of their five children, on a council site where they have taken over the

Picture 100: Jason Clee and young Violet's daughter Donna in 2006

lease and manage it. Donna and Stacey Marie live at the Hopton site in Stafford and Bridie Kate lives on a private site in Cannock with her in-laws. Violet has seven grandchildren. She is looking forward to their holiday over Easter with many of her family off to Spain for a week.

Dawn and Joyce didn't have far to travel as they both live in Stafford.

Dawn is retired and lives in a house on Stafford Common with her husband Harry who still works selling carpets as well as conducting the traditional Gypsy trades of tarmacking, gardening and collecting scrap and

Picture 101: Joyce, Miselli and Dawn, Glover Street March 20th 2016

rags. They have four children and 11 grandchildren. One of Dawn's daughters, Leanne, lives nearby in a rented house though she still takes to the road in her trailer. Dawn's other children are scattered elsewhere some in houses and others in trailers. Henry and Zillah and their families live on council sites in Peterborough and Oxford and Baby Dawn lives on a private site in Evesham. Zillah's sons Tommy, Harry and Ned are very keen and talented lightweight boxers with the British Amateur Boxing Association (BABA) and have won many championships and awards.

Joyce rents a house in Doxey with her son Riley. Her other children are scattered with her daughter Baby Joyce living in Market Harborough on her own site and Billy Joe, Wayne, Riley and Leslie James living on private sites in Gloucester and Pershore. Between them they have given Zillah 17 great grandchildren and 5 great great grandchildren.

Baby Joyce's three boys, Lucky Boy, Ben and Cole are also boxers and compete in British Amateur Boxing Association national and international championships. Ben has won in world events twice and had the Golden Gloves. Cole begins fighting in the British Amateur Boxing Association championships in May. Baby Joyce herself goes to combat lessons every morning.

Picture 102: Dawn's grandchildren Tommy, Harry and Ned 2003

Zillah's oldest son Ivor and his wife Violet have also been living near Zillah since 2000 in a house in Doxey, Stafford. Their six children live

in trailers on various Gypsy sites throughout the Midlands. Ivor, their eldest, and Debbie their youngest live with their family on Ivor's own site in Much Wenlock in Shropshire. Violet, their eldest daughter, lives with her four children George, Alan, Mary Louise and Luke and two small grandchildren at the Fishponds site next to the field where Zillah herself lived with Ivor before he died. Still located between Penkridge and Wolverhampton and opposite Featherstone prison, it is now owned by Hubert, the

Picture 103: Joyce's daughter Baby Joyce 2011

Picture 104: Joyce's grandson Lucky Boy Lee with his British ABA trophies 2011

Picture 105: Joyce's grandsons Ben Lee with younger brother Cole and Granddad 2011

grand nephew of Zillah's husband Ivor (Hubert is the son of Slatter and Olivine who was Ivor's sister). The other children of Ivor and Violet live with their families on a private site in Doncaster (Andrew), a flat near Manchester (Billy) and a council site in King's Winsford (Samantha).

Zillah's son Ivor as well as other members of the extended Smith family attend the Life and Light Gypsy Traveller Churches in Willenhall and Rugeley and sometimes attend conventions, which are held in enormous tents, across the United Kingdom and France.

Joey Varey, Mary's widower also lives not far from Zillah in a house in Doxey and continues with the traditional Gypsy occupations of horse-trading, tarmacking, gardening and scrap collecting. He has a caravan at the back of his house. He and Mary had four daughters, Mary, Sharon, Joanne and Suzie, 15 grandchildren and six great grandchildren. Their girls all have Gypsy Traveller husbands and all live in their own houses in a row near their father. The eldest, Mary, has two daughters who live at the back of her house in trailers. The grandchildren all went to Doxey Primary school but did not go on to secondary school. This was due to the fear of the parents and the children themselves of them being corrupted and losing their childhood.

Not far from Stafford Zillah's second eldest son Tony, his wife Sheila and their three girls and a boy have lived on their own land for 30 years in bungalows at the Hopton Caravan site next to a Gorgia

caravan site. There were the usual problems of getting a license at first but their right to stay there is all settled now and they don't go to the Feathersone site any more. Tony has his own carpet warehouse business. All their children, Sheila, Tammy, Tony and Suzie went to Hopton Primary school. They gave Zillah 10 grandchildren. Some children go to the local school in Weston and the others are home tutored about once a fortnight by the local Traveller Education Support Service (TESS).

Picture 106: Violet's grandchildren, Indiana, Jason Jeremiah, James Dean and Tiana.

Alan and Julie have also settled on the Hopton site for the past ten years after travelling around the country up north to Doncaster and then back down to Liverpool and as far south as Exeter. Alan sells carpets and beds as well as the traditional Gypsy occupations. They used to go to Wales in the summer. Now with their four children, Chantelle, Alan, Nathan and Georgia and their seven grandchildren, they tend to go abroad for holidays in a large family group with Julie as the main organizer. However, next week for a change she and Alan are going by themselves to the Gran Canarias.

They love the Hopton site, which they say is "lovely and in the countryside" The grandchildren will go to the local primary school at Hopton but Julie thinks they will not go on to secondary school. Though she says if they want to they will as "nowadays

Picture 107: Zillah and Julie at Glover Street March 20th 2016

times are changing and that generation seem to want to further their education."

Nathan, Julie and Alan's youngest son keeps very fit and he and his brother Alan are keen runners who, in 2005, crossed the Stafford half marathon finish line together with a time of just 1 hour and 30 minutes. The money they raised was part of their families support for Macmillan Cancer Relief. Alan went on to run the London Marathon

Picture 108: Alan, the son of Alan and Julie, October 2006

for Katharine House Stafford and in 2006 he ran in the New York marathon to raise £1200 for Get Kids Going, which provides support and mobility aids to disabled children. Alan's wife Joanne is a world travelled English Gypsy whose family are scattered in Canada, Ireland, Australia and England. Zillah attended their wedding in Ireland with other family members a few years ago. Zillah had already experienced flying in her 70s when she went on holiday to Tenerife with Joyce and her family. Zillah thoroughly enjoyed herself on that occasion and told some fortunes to holidaymakers over there.

Sharon, John's widow also lives on the Hopton site with her family: Jodie with two boys and a girl; Michaela with two boys and a girl; Jade with one girl; and John with two boys and a girl. Sharon's eldest, Sharon Marie, lives in Sandbach with her in-laws and her three girls and a boy so that her second eldest Shinia can attend a special school. The rest of Zillah's great grandchildren go to the local primary schools. The eldest grandchild did not go to the secondary school due to the parents' fear of possible corruption.

Ronnie married Michelle who is both Gypsy and Gorgia and they used to live on Glover Street with Zillah in the 1990s but now they rent a house at Doxey near two of their children Hayley Michelle,

Picture 109: Michelle Smith, Ronnie's daughter, and her husband, Richard in 2005

Adam and their families. Their other daughter Tina Marie and her family live on a private site at Brierly Hill and their son Ronnie with his family lives on a private site in Gloucester. Between them they gave Zillah seven grandchildren.

Tooney Neggick, the widower of Zillah's daughter Tina Marie, rents a house in Willenhall with his son Tooney who is a roofer. Young Tina Marie a hairdresser and young mother of a toddler, Jacob, lives in a house in Willenhall with her Gorgia husband Garnet Jackson who is an electrician.

Grace travelled from Temple Grafton a small village near Stratford-upon-Avon. She and her husband Riley Smith continue their struggle to have their site registered as an official site. The Smith family have lived in that area of Worcester for 25 years and bought the land five years ago solely for the use of their own family (Grace and Riley's four adult children, Grace, Riley, Herbert and Dean, their spouses and 11 grandchildren) to ensure they had a permanent base for the children to go to school. Since then the grandchildren have been able to attend the local

Picture 110: Rita, Grace, Zillah and Violet, Glover Street, March 20th 2016

school and have done very well belonging to numerous school clubs. The school has a good reputation for educating Gypsy children and seven of the children were still currently at the local school and were very happy there. Abigail loves the secondary school but her three siblings did not settle there and are being home tutored by the local Traveller Education Service once every 4 to 6 weeks.

Grace and Riley obtained a temporary license in 2012 due for renewal in 2015. Some local residents had begun raising objections because they thought the site spoilt the view when they were walking in the nearby countryside. Their future had become once again very uncertain. With the use of a law firm with years of experience representing Gypsies, and with support from the local community they felt they had a good case for the planning permission to be made permanent. Letters from the local school and the church were sent to the parish and planning committee councilors in support of their application. The letters explained how they were a very highly respected family in the Gypsy Community who were working hard at bettering themselves under their own terms. They were self-employed, paid their taxes and used the site as a base from which they could continue their travelling lifestyle during the summer visiting families in other parts of the Midlands and doing seasonal work.

It was also pointed out that Grace and Riley needed their site as a base to which they can return and thereby give the family a security, which enabled them to have a sustainable Gypsy lifestyle. At the same time they had also become part of the Temple Grafton village community by being active members of the church and taking part in church and village events. They were granted another temporary licence in March 2015.

The consensus amongst Zillah's children is that things were better years ago. The days of fruit picking holidays are over. Nearly all the plum orchards in Worcestershire have been pulled up for wheat fields and the strawberries and blackcurrants are picked by machine, workers from abroad or Gorgias picking their own. Morals are more lax and children are addicted to TV, videos, computers and phones yet they still get bored. There are fewer places to stay and they are only allowed to stay on council sites, which are few and far between. Obtaining licences for private sites on their own land is very difficult and expensive. The Romany language is dying out. Yet despite all the enormous social changes and upheavals throughout this and the last century, the story of Zillah and her extended family give us all hope. Their survival illustrates the power of resourcefulness and optimism. They support each other, keep alive family stories and memories and maintain strict moral codes. All this has enabled them to continue surviving in a house dwelling society with their identity intact.

Appendix 2

Zillah's Romany Jib Glossary

Bal – hair
Balovas – bacon
Bender – tent
Bengs – devils
Buriker – town

Cannie – chicken
Chav /chavvies – child/ children
Chinger – to fight
Chockes – shoes
Chore – take
Cushini – basket

Dadus – father
Daia – mother
Didakai – Gypsy friend, rough traveller
Dordi – dear me
Dray – cart
Drom – road
Dukker – tell fortunes

Fence – sell

Gav – village or town
Gavver – police officer
Gorgi – female house dweller
Gorgio – house dweller (male or female)
Grai – horse
Granted – blessed

Hawking – selling from door to door
Hobin – shopping
Hoggies, Hochis – hedgehogs

Jell – go
Jen – give
Jib – language
Jukkel – dog

Kosh – stick
Kushti – nice

Lell – catch
Lova – money

Marikli – cake
Mass – meat
Mokadi – unclean
Mong – beg
Monushi – woman
Morra – bread
Mulla – the devil, to kill, corpse
Mush – man

Pabs – apples
Parnny – water
Parry – wash
Povengros – potatoes
Puridad – grandfather
Putch – ask
Puv – field

Rakli – non-Gypsy girl
Rawni – woman
Rocka – to speak , to tell
Rom – husband/Romany man
Romni – wife
Rai – gentleman

Scran – food
Shoshes – rabbits

Trarty – tomorrow
Tud – milk
Tugers – clothes
Tuvlers – cigarettes

Varda – horse drawn waggon or caravan
Val – hair
Valervess – bacon

Woodrus – bed

Yog – fire
Yorros – eggs

Appendix 3

Family Poems

We'll Meet Again

Last New Year's Eve
I'll remember forever.
We were in my brother and sister in law's trailer,
Dempsey, Ida, Joey, Mary and me.
Mary wanted it.
The men were having a drink
And Joey was playing the mouth organ.
I said to Mary, "Sing us a song".
"No", she replied "I can't."

So I sang her a song
While Ida went for the coal.
I sang "It's only make believe"
And an Irish song nobody knows only me.
Then a cowboy song as I used to be a lovely yodeller.
This time I couldn't yodel,
Though they said I sang lovely.
Ida asked me to tap dance and I did that well too.

I said, "Go on Mary give us a song".
"Alright Mam", she replied, "just one for you".

She sang us "We'll meet again some sunny day"
And now she's gone.

We're all hurt and can't believe she's dead.
She was such a beautiful person.
Joey says he won't live long.
"When I'm down there in the earth
With my lovely wife I'll be alright"

All the family are desolated. Deeply shocked.

The week after her death I began to hear her singing
so beautifully. "We'll meet again , don't know where, don't know when,
but we will meet again some sunny day".

Mary and her sister sing to me in the morning and at night.
You'll never witness sounds so beautiful
as the yodelling song with Tina Marie
in harmony and music with it.
The more I listened the louder it got
like angels singing to me.
They sang to me about Jesus on the cross
who said, "I'll never leave you.
I'll always be there. Touch the ground."

Mary sang "Touch the ground Mam,
Jesus is with me. I'll always be there."

This means when I go to her grave
I'll touch the ground.

Zillah Smith (2006)

Dad

Dad it's an honour and privilege to be your son.
I don't always' thank you for what you have done.
We've spent much time through the years
laughing, joking, sometimes tears.

We know each other inside out.
Though sometimes we just want to shout.
But it's not hard for people to see
I love you and you love me.

And after all is said and done
No one knows the father like the son.
I love you Dad.
Your son John Joseph

John Joseph Smith (2015)

John

Last night in dreams
I saw your face,
I felt the warmth of your embrace.
My mind turns back the hands of time
when we was all happy
and things was fine.
Now you have gone
but not far away
'cause in my heart my loving brother
you will live each day.
God bless you.
Grace

Grace Smith (2015)

Uncle John

God needed an angel up above
so he called you up with all his love.
Now the Lord keeps you in his warm embrace
but we just want to see your smiling face.
John we miss you with all our hearts
'cause now we all have been pulled apart.
Now you're in the Heavenly skies.
You're with our Lord way up high.
You watch us and keep us safe at night.
When you were with us everything was right.
You're the one we want to see.
We all loved you.
You was part of our family.
God Bless.
Abbie

Abigail Birch, aged 12 (2015)

Picture 111: Tony, Alan, Zillah, John and Ronnie March 20th 2015

The Gavvers have rocked we have to jell trarty
(The police have said we have to go tomorrow)

The gavvers has rocked we have to jell trarty
We'll jell down the drum with the vardas and grais.
We'll hatch on the side of the drum.
The mushes will chore the grais in the puv and jen them some parnny.

The mushes are jelling over the puves with the jukkels
to lell some shoshes and dick for a kosh to mulla the hoggies with.
Rocka the chavies to lell a bit of kosh to make a yog.

We'll jell down the gav to hawk the cares
We'll fence all the cushinis to lell a bit of lova
And dick for a kushti rackli to dukke,
mong for a few tugers and chockes
We'll go to the buriker to get a bit of hobin.
Putch the rakli for some morra, tud and tuvlers,
yorros, a cannie, bit of mass, some balovas
a bag of povengros and pabs.

Then jell back to vardas with the hobin.
Lell the chavvies the scran then parry the chavvies
Wash their bal and jell them to woodrus and then we can
parry them few tugers.

Zillah Smith

The Police have said we have to go tomorrow

The Police have said we have to go tomorrow
So we'll go down the road with the wagons and horses.
We'll pull on the roadside
The men will put the horses in the field and give them some water

The men can take the dogs over the fields
and catch some rabbits and look for a stick to kill the hedgehogs with
Tell the children to get some sticks to make a fire

The women will go down the town to call the houses
To sell all the baskets to the women for a bit of money
And look for a nice girl to tell her fortune
beg a few clothes and shoes

Then we'll go to the shop to get a bit of shopping,
ask the woman for a loaf of bread , milk and fags
eggs, a chicken, some meat, a bag of potatoes and apples.

Then go back to the wagons with the shopping,
Give the children the food, then wash their hair
Put them to bed and then wash those few clothes.

Translated by Grace Smith

Gypsies Live with Nature

Relaxing on the grass, under the cool blue sky,
whistling with the birds from way up high
Gypsies live with nature.

Climbing up the huge towering trees,
collecting fresh water from the flowing stream,
Gypsies live with nature.

Never giving the lovely animals a fright,
we would never hurt this wonderful sight.
Gypsies live with nature.

We love the environment. We respect the land.
We love the world as if it was in the palm of our hand.
Gypsies live with nature.

Our beautiful world we would never pollute.
Instead of ruining it we care and salute.
Gypsies live with nature.

We treat nature just like our friends.
This undying love will never end.
Gypsies live with nature

Abbie Birch aged 11 (2014)

Granny Grace

Granny you are so fine
Granny you've loved me a long time
Granny you take us to the park
Granny you shush the dogs when they do bark
Granny you love the girls and boys
Granny you give us lots of toys
Granny you are the best at cooking
Granny your eyes sparkle when you are looking
Granny you come with us in the car
Granny you are a beautiful star
That's what you are

Abbie Birch aged 8 (2011)

Appendix 4

Family stories

The Gypsy Boy and the Mulla

Zillah Smith

As years gone by there was me dad's great puridad (great grandfather). And this is what he told my puridad and he told my father. The old people used to use those old Romany words for mam and dad and granddad in them days. Anyway me dad's great puridad once knew a Gypsy boy. This boy and 'is family was all up this lane about three or four mile from a village and there wasn't a house in sight nor nothin'. An' this young Gypsy boy he wanted some money an' 'is daia and dadus (mother and father) wouldn't give 'im none. An' he used to play a fiddle.

They wouldna give 'im none an' said, "No we don't want you goin' to the pub an' goin' off and leaving the Gypsy vardas. The devil himself sent beer into the world." They wanted him to stop there an' not get into any mischief or get anythin' happen to him.

So he said, "If you don't give me no money," 'e said, and kept on an' on. He was cryin' an' they wouldn't give 'im none, (because they never had none hardly to give him). An' he said, "If you don't give me no money daia and dada I'm gonna pray to the Mulla (Devil)."

So his Dadus said, "You're not gettin' no money an' anyroad too much money is a bad thing; it is the road to hell. You'll never get to heaven at this rate."

"Well," he said, "I'm goin' to the public. Why should I go to heaven anyroad? Isn't heaven full o' bavel (wind) an' snow an' hailstones? I'm too young. They're all greybeards in heaven. I'm for the Mulla with his bugle blasts an' hounds an' wine!"

Well he started walkin' down this lane an' he got half way down it and he sat on a stile an' he started playin' his fiddle. And he said he'd play for the Devil an' he did. He kept playin all his tunes, you know like they used to play sometimes in the pub, and they'd give 'em sixpence or a penny or whatever it was in them days.

So he started playin' up this lane an' this big gentleman come along. He was dressed up like a real rai (gentleman). And the boy thought he was a gentleman. He didn't think of what he had said that he'd play to the devil. 'Cos he'd be terrified of 'im. He only said it in temper because he couldn't get no money.

An' this big rai, he 'ad a big top hat on and a big one o' them coats like a swallowtail coat you know. An' these trousers. Only he throwed 'im some money in 'is hat. It wasn't a little bit neither. It was a good bit o' money he throwed in, all silver. Throwed it in 'is hat.

So he kept on playin', an' he was playin' an' the rai said, "You can come up to my 'ouse?".

"I don't think so," he says, "I might go to the pub."

So the Gypsy boy kept playin' an' this gentleman went past an' he didn't take no notice of 'im. He kept playin'. So after he 'ad this money he played an' there was nobody else to come down there was there? Because nobody'd be walkin' down there 'cos it was too far away. So he went to the pub. An' when he gorrin the pub he was tellin' his friends he had a gentleman give him some money. An' he gor his drink or whatever he wanted an' he started playin' his fiddle in there. An' then he seen this gentleman and said, "There's the gentleman what give me the money," to the other Gypsy boys.

An' they said, "Ooh is that 'im?" An' one of 'em looked an' his hair lifted his hat from his head. He cried out, "Aw Dordi! Dordi! That's the Mulla! You've played to the Mulla," he said, "an' he'll 'ave yer."

The Gypsy boy said, "Gerraway! Don't talk silly!"

"Well have a look at 'is shoes an' his tail. He got a tail under that coat."

And he had a cloven foot an' it was like a cow's foot, you know what I mean? An' his other foot was like a grai's foot.

"You've played to the Mulla. He'll 'ave yer. You've sold yer soul to him now so it's no good you botherin' about it. You took 'is money an' you played to 'im, an' you said you'd play to the Devil. You said you'd sell your soul.

The Gypsy boy said, "Don't talk silly. No such thing. Can't be. There's no such thing."

So he went home this young man and he didn't take no notice of it. Thought they was only messin' about foolin' him y'know. Though all the other lads wouldna go wid 'im. They was frightened. They don't like anythin' like that about the Devil. They don't like to mention about the Mulla. But in them days I s'pose it was true.

So when he went 'ome he told his daia and dadus an' he said, "I got some money," he said, "an' I went to the pub."

They said, "I bet you've done it now, haven't yer? Yer too old for us to blow into your ears any longer! Playin' to the devil." They said, "Playin' to the Mulla to get money. Bet he comes for you! Yer nothin' but a big puddin' with nothin' in it!"

"Gerroff!"he said and got to bed in a little varda of his own you know wid his brothers. So they all was in bed an' it must've been sometime in the mornin'.

This mush, this big rai, this gentleman, that s'pose to be a gentleman comes to the door an' he says, "I want my rights."

The Gypsy boy was frightened. Shiverin' in bed he was! He said, "Who's that? Go away!" he said. "We're all in bed. There's nobody 'ere."

The rai said, "I want my rights."

"What rights?"

"You're the one what played to me aren't yer? I want my soul," he said.

"Your soul!" An' he was shiverin' in bed an' his dadus an' his daia were almost frightened t'death.

So he said, "No I'm not comin'."

"You can come with me," he said, " an' I'll tell you what I'll do. You can come to my big 'ouse," he said, " an' play for all our people. An' you'll 'ave loads o'money like that," he said.

"No, I'm not comin'."

So he grabbed 'im out an' took 'im.

There was no 'ouse in this lane, no nothin. An' when he was goin' up this road, takin' him over this field it was like lights, an' all 'ouses. Like a big castle thing an' all lights goin' up it, y'know, like lights burnin'.

Well he took him up there an' he said, "Now you can come an' play for all my people," he said. "An' you play lovely," he said, "an' you're very clever with yer music. If you play fer all them you'll 'ave plenty o'money," he said. "You'll go outa this castle with loads o' money in yer pocket. That much money yer can't carry."

"No, I don' wanna play, I don' wanna play," 'cos he knowed what he done. He was frightened.

"You've got t'play, an' I'll take you in."

An' when he got in the castle, there was more like him, big gentlemen, an' there was loads o' little imps dancin'up an' down, all dancin' an' runnin' up an' down.

The old man, his dadus, he went there to look where his son was an' he couldn't see no places or no 'ouses. They knowed he took 'im over the field but he couldn't find him. He couldn't do nothin' about it. He said, "He's took 'im. We won't see 'im no more now."

Anyway the Mulla made him play an' he played an' he played till all hours in the mornin'. An' when he finished playin' a lot o' these little imps all went. The Mulla made 'em all vanish but the ole Devil he was still there.

He give 'im all this money an' he said, "You can go 'ome now with all this money." The Gypsy boy was glad he could go home but he said, "I don't want no money, you can keep it."

So what his daia done before he went out an' after he said he'd play to the devil, she put a coat there with no pockets in, she cut them all out so the money wouldn't stop in, whatever they give 'im. 'Cos if he had the money it'd be worse for 'im. She cut holes in his pocket an' nowhere to put it. The Mulla kept putting it in an' the boy said, "I don't want no money you Devil Mulla are a poor mush. You 'ave no soul. I'm a rich mush - I've still got mine an' you anna havin' it!"

But it was no use. The boy went walkin' an' as he was walkin' there was all these great big fires an' all these bengs an' devils dancin' round it. The hellhounds were athirst and the Mulla had found them something to drink. An the big devil gentleman what took 'im said, "Now you can go down there an' you can go 'ome."

An' they all cutch 'old of 'im an they ripped 'im an' ripped 'im from pillar t'post an' throwed 'im on this fire with all his clothes an' ripped 'im up an' made 'im play an' made 'im play an' made 'im play till all the fire 'ad nearly burnt out. An' after that they throwed 'im on the fire. They'd killed 'im. An' that was the end of it.

When all the Gypsies went to look for him, they got the police t'look for me dadus's great puridad's friend's son. He had an idea, me dadus's great puridad. He had an idea they wouldn't find 'im, 'cos the other Gypsies told him. They said, "We've seen 'im. It was the Mulla. He played to him an' he come in the pub 'cos he wanted to foller 'im an' he knew where he was an' he wanted to give him more money, an' he put more money in his pocket an' he never took no notice of it."

So when you do sell your soul to the devil, the devil has your soul. They do what they want with you an' then they burn you. They do honestly. They did in them days."

My Life as a Gypsy

Abigail Birch Age 10

My name is Abigail. I am a Gypsy. I live in a caravan with my Mam and Dad and two sisters. We live at Temple Grafton on our own Gypsy site. We are very good with animals especially horses and dogs. My granny Grace has a horse who is a shire called Misty and I have a dog called Copper. I like living here because you never get lonely, because all my cousins live next to us.

At school I have many friends, who live in houses. They also don't care if I am a Gypsy or not. My life is very different to theirs but I still love the Gypsy life. I enjoy taking Copper, and the other dogs, on long walks with Granny in the summer with my cousins, aunties, uncles, and granny and grandad. As well as this we also have lots of animals. My granddad has lots of chickens. and more dogs. Finally we also have cats to get rid of mice and rats.

Every Sunday, if it's on, we all go to church. I like it there because everyone excepts (sic) our differences and treats us like everyone else. The way we should. They except(sic) us for who we are, that is perfect.

At school me and my cousins are the only Gypsies. I love going to school to see all my friends. My best friend at school, Kayla, and me are very different. Such as she lives in a house and I live in a caravan and other reasons too but we don't let that get in the way of our friendship.

Living here is very fun because of all the beautiful emerald green fields in the summer. My granny sometimes tells us what she used to eat when she was little, like seeds and blackberries she gathered. What also makes it fun is we have our own special language that my granny is teaching us. It is very unique and that's what makes us special. Granny teaches us Romany talk like juckle means dog. Gypsies still have horses and carts but all of us live day to day in caravans.

Christmas is my best time of year because all of us get to spend time as one big family. We don't forget the presents. I love being a Gypsy and I never want life to change. I think being a Gypsy makes us special and I love that. We are different to others in our own way. We are individual and that is what matters!

Our Gypsy life in AMAZING!

Appendix 5

Stafford Chronicle Friday August 9th 1996

Travelling tradition nearing a standstill, says Zillah

Amber Henshaw meets up with one of the last of a dying breed.... The Romanys

ZILLAH Boswell is a remarkable woman, not only has she got 70 grandchildren and 36 great grandchildren, she is also a Romany gipsy

At 72 years old Zillah has spent her life travelling around Britain but has always returned to Stafford periodically.

Although she still travels, a little less frequently than she used to, she is based for most of the time now at a council gipsy site in the town.

The life of travellers is probably something that us house dwellers have difficulty understanding or appreciating.

In the same way gipsies possibly don't understand our desire to live in the same place.

But the life of Romanys has changed dramatically in Zillah's lifetime.

She said: "We stopped using our horse and caravan about 40 years ago but a lot of Romany people have still got them."

She said that in the early days they were able to stop on land without it being a problem.

She said that they could always use common land then but now even that is all fenced up.

She said: "They used to let us stop and then if they wanted to they would tell us to move, it was not as bad then as it is now."

Zillah guesses that their are thousands of Romanys living in Britain now, most of them live on specially allocated council sites.

Her life is probably closer now to that of house dwellers than she ever imagined.

She said: "We have to stick to the site because if we move then someone else can take our space.

"We haven't got the Romany freedom anymore.

"They should make it so we can move on to another site every three months, otherwise we are like house dwellers.

"I like house dwellers very much though, I always have done.

"I think they are very good. You get a few bad ones and you get a few bad gipsies, it is the same on either side."

It is not only the travelling side of Romany life that has changed during the years but also how they make their living.

In the old days gipsies used to make flowers, baskets and pegs to sell to house dwellers, but then the shops took over.

Romanys are also reknowned for their psychic sense and ability to see into the future, but now people are able to go off and learn how to read tarots, palms and feet.

She said: "Travelling people like myself, they had the gift born in them.

"I went to school but I can't read or write most of my family can't, but they all go to school."

To make their money now Romanys do jobs for house dwellers, collect scrap and some of the younger ones even work in factories. Zillah said: "We have a hard life sometimes we have not known which way to turn.

"The young ones are going to find it more difficult."

Endnotes

1   Varda - wagon or caravan. The word varda originates from the Iranian word "vurdun". They were highly valued but Gypsies rarely made their own. They were commissioned from specialised Gorgio coach builders. It took between 6 and 12 months to build a varda using oak, ash, elm, walnut and pine. They were then painted and decorated ornately with carvings, and often goldleaf.

2   Jumping the broomsticks is a phrase and custom relating to a wedding ceremony where the couple jumps over a broom to validate through their own custom an otherwise non-legally binding or non-church wedding. The custom is historically associated with the Romany people of the United Kingdom, especially those in Wales (Thompson, T. W. "British Gipsy Marriage and Divorce Rites", quoted in The Times, Issue 54004, 21 September 1928; p.11.) A paper read at the 1928 jubilee congress of the Folk Lore Society in London refers to this: "In Wales there was preserved until recently a marriage ritual of which the central feature was the jumping of the bride and bridegroom over a branch of flowering broom or over a besom made of broom."

3   A stove manufactured by Smith and Wellstood called the Queen Anne or 'Queenie' for short. It has its origins in the late 19th century and remained in production up until the 1940s. They were commonly used in Gypsy caravans but were also used in many other applications like offices, parlours, narrow boats, showman vans etc.

4   Historically, these Welsh 'double-cloth' or tapestry blankets were woven from two-ply woollen yarn on primitive hand-looms. The weaving involved many shafts and treadles working together to produce two interlocking fabrics woven simultaneously. Materials used were untreated wool using natural dyes including madder and cochineal for reds, woad and indigo for blues and various berries and lichens for other shades and tints. In rural Wales, almost every home, including those of Gypsies' possessed these

blankets. They came to symbolise hearth and home and their hard-wearing texture meant that they could be utilized for a range of things from rugs and curtains to bed coverings. Importantly, they were also made as family heirlooms and often given as wedding gifts as part of a girl's dowry. They were considered as precious belongings to be handed down from one generation to another. The Blodwen Heritage Blanket Project http://www.blodwen. com/blodwens_community.php

5   The Battle of Le Cateau was essentially a rearguard action fought by the British in late August 1914, during the general Allied retreat along the Western Front in the face of sustained German successes at the four Battles of the Frontier. http://www. firstworldwar.com/battles/lecateau.htm

6   Gypsy Step Dancing https://www.youtube.com/ watch?v=OTclrg5g97g

7   The Romani people in Spain are generally known as gitanos.

8   https://mainlynorfolk.info/folk/records/thevoiceofthepeople. html

9   "The Longest Furrow: a Countryman's Reflections on Rural Life Volume 1 by Frederick Charles Waterfall (Owd Fred) a Stafford Farmer. Fred Waterfall Publications 2009 mail@fcwaterfall.co.uk

Further Reading List

Acton, T., (ed), *Gypsy Politics and Traveller Identity*, University of Hertfordshire Press, Hatfield, 1997.

Acton, T. and Mundy, G., *Romani Culture and Gypsy Identity*, University of Hertfordshire Press, Hatfield, 1997.

Adams, B. et al., *Gypsies and Government Policy in England*, Heinemann, London, 1975.

Bhopa, K. et al., *Working Towards Inclusive Education: aspects of good practice for Gypsy Traveller children*, DfEE/HMSO, London, Research Report No. 238, 2000.

Churches Commission for Racial Justice, *Gypsies, Travellers and the Church*, June 1998.

Hawes, D. and Perez, B, *The Gypsy and the State: The Ethnic Cleansing of British Society*, The Policy Press, Bristol, 2nd edition, 1996.

Jarman, E. and Jarman, A. O. H., *The Welsh Gypsies*, Cardiff University of Wales Press 1991.

Kenrick, D., and Clark, C. *Moving On: The Gypsies and Travellers of Britain*, University of Hertfordshire Press, Hatfield, 1999.

Kenrick, D. and Puxon, G., *Gypsies Under the Swastika* University of Hertfordshire Press, Hatfield, 1 Jan 2009

Morris, R. and Clements, L. (eds), *Gaining Ground: Law reform for Gypsies and Travellers*, University of Hertfordshire Press, Hatfield, 1999.

Persaud, T., Christianity Thrives among Gypsies Despite Prejudice. Roma Revival: Missionary efforts continue to succeed, in *Christianity Today*, Nov 2010, Vol. 54, No 11, Pg 15.

Pinnock, K., (ed), et al., *Denied a Future? The Right to Education of Roma/ Gypsy and Traveller Children in Europe*, Save The Children, London, 2001.

Quarmby, K., *No Place To Call Home: Inside The Real Lives Of Gypsies And Travellers*, Oneworld Publications. 22 Aug 2013.

Richardson, J. and Andrew Ryder (eds.) *Gypsies and Travellers: Empowerment and Inclusion in British Society*, Policy Press. September 2012.

Thurfjell, D. and Marsh., (eds) *Romani Pentecostalism: Gypsies and Charismatic Christianity*, Peter Lang, 2014.

Waterson, M., "I want more than green leaves for my children: some developments in Gypsy/Traveller education, 1970-1996", in Acton, T. and Mundy, G. (eds), *Romani Culture and Gypsy Identity*, University of Hertfordshire Press, Hatfield, 1997.

Webster, L., *The Impact of the Criminal Justice and Public Order Act on the Lives of Travellers and their Children*, A Report for the Children's Society, June 1995.

Weiss-Wendt, A., *The Nazi Genocide of the Roma: Reassessment and Commemoration*, Berghahn Books, 1 May 2015

About the Author

Netta Cartwright, a graduate of Aberystwyth, Cardiff, Keele and Birmingham Universities, is a school counselling trainer with 30 years school teaching and 20 years school counselling experience. She was a founder member of Stafford Women's Aid and was equal opportunities advisor for Staffordshire LEA where she promoted anti-racist and anti-sexist projects in schools. Netta leads peer support courses in the UK and abroad in primary and secondary schools in the public and private sector. Her publications include: "Towards Bully Free Schools: Interventions in Action" (OUP); "Peer Support Works: a Step by Step Guide to Long Term Success" (Network Continuum); and many articles in educational journals. Her work in schools has been featured on Channel 4 and BBC1. Netta is the secretary of "There is No Planet B" a voluntary group that organises Stafford's Annual Green Arts Festival. In September 2015 she founded the Stafford Welcomes Refugees voluntary group and is its chairperson.

Picture 112: Netta, Zillah and Grace June 17th 2016

About the Editor

The late Dr Katherine Mulraney (nee Pinnock), Netta's daughter, was a graduate of Nottingham Trent and Wolverhampton Universities, where she went on to complete her doctoral thesis. The subject of her PhD was the situation of Roma in Bulgaria where she worked voluntarily for Roma Non Governmental Organisations. Subsequently she worked for Save the Children where she coordinated the "Denied a Future" project, which produced the first analysis of the rights and access to education of Roma, Gypsy and Traveller children across Europe. After editing and co- writing "Denied a Future" she was interviewed on national news programmes. At Birmingham University Kath worked on The National Evaluation of the Children's Fund (NECF) that ran from January 2003 to March 2006. As Senior Research Fellow at the Policy Research Institute, University of Wolverhampton, Kath evaluated the Staffordshire Children's Fund. Her most recent work for GHK Consulting Ltd (now ICF International) was leading the evaluation of the government's pilot Universal Credit scheme and identifying the many ways it could be improved. Kath used research and evaluation to improve life for vulnerable and disadvantaged groups, especially children and young people. She remained committed to the Roma cause. Shortly before she passed away after a long illness on September 1st 2016 she had completed the editing of this book.

Picture 113: Zillah and Katherine March 20th 2016

18869116R00084

Printed in Great Britain
by Amazon